AWAKEN
THE DARK HORSE PROPHET

ISBN: 9798645346409

Cover design by David Joseph

A Publication of Tall Pine Books

|| *tallpinebooks.com*

*Printed in the United States of America

AWAKEN
THE DARK HORSE PROPHET

JENNIFER MARTIN

TALL PINE

"Jennifer's new book: *Awaken*, is going to take you on a prophet's journey through a series of unfolding dreams and revelations to help equip your faith and perspective for what God is doing for you. This book is filled with spiritual insight that can connect some deep hope for what God wants to do with you and for the world. She has a great sense of developing the prophetic narrative of her experiences with her prophetic understanding and you are going to be glad you read her book!"

—SHAWN BOLZ
Host of *Exploring the Prophetic Podcast* & *Translating God* TV show
Author of *Translating God, Provision: Prophecies, Prayers, and Declarations, & Keys to Heaven's Economy*
www.bolzministries.com

"*Awaken: The Dark Horse Prophet* is a wonderful book written to encourage prophets and intercessors who are unknown and unrecognized by the body of Christ, but called by God to the harvest fields by God himself. Another Great Awakening is breaking on the earth even now and Jennifer Martin has written a book that feels like a heartfelt and intimate letter to a few of her closest friends to stay the course God has set them on until His intentions in them and through them are fully manifested in this world. God has many sons and daughters, who few consider significant, that He intends to use mightily in these last days. You may be a dark horse in this race, but run your race to win."

—JOAN HUNTER
Author/Healing Evangelist
Host of *Miracles Happen!* TV show

"Jennifer Martin is a prophetess...a dreamer, whom God has entrusted Kingdom secrets and mysteries to. In her book, *Awaken: The Dark Horse Prophet*, she shares a number of prophetic dreams and encounters that reveal important messages for this hour. We need to know what the Spirit of God is saying to the church. Jennifer Martin is called to help give you valuable insight and direction for this coming season."

—PATRICIA KING
Author, Minister, Television Host
www.patriciaking.com

"Jennifer Martin's book, *Awaken: The Dark Horse Prophet,* is an incredible deep well that is overflowing with the revelation from the heart of God for this new era. As I read each page, I felt the refreshing waters of His Spirit crashing over me and I could feel the tangible impartation of hope, faith, divine clarity, insight and wisdom of God being released. Can I encourage you as you journey through these pages, take it slowly, meditate on the words penned here by the Holy Spirit through Jennifer as I believe that this book will not only refresh you, breathe life into you, release hope to you and increase hunger in you to encounter Jesus in a deeper way, but it will position you in greater ways to partner with this 'never seen before', incredible move of His Spirit that is upon us and the earth."

—LANA VAWSER
Prophetic Voice, Itinerant Speaker *Lana Vawser Ministries*
Author of *The Prophetic Voice of God & A Time to Selah*
www.lanavawser.com

"Jennifer Martin is not only one of my dearest friends, she is an incredible prophetic voice in this generation. Her book, *Awaken: The Dark Horse Prophet*, is so powerful and timely in this season. It is a manifesto for those who long for a personal prophetic awakening and inspiration to partake of the dark horse movement. I encourage you to get your hands on this book!"

—BRYNN SHAMP

Co-Founder & Executive Director

Destiny Encounters International

"Not only are Jennifer and Munday Martin great friends of mine, but they are intimate friends of Jesus. Wow!! This book is fresh and articulate! The picture Jennifer paints when she writes leaves you hungry for more as she opens and unfolds such beauty through simple truths. The revelation is laid out in such symbolic practical application much of which has been born through visions and dreams. Again...Wow! I highly recommend this book for those who are hungry to encounter the Lord in a profound way."

—JEFF JANSEN

Global Fire Ministries International

Senior Leader *Global Fire Church*

Author of *Glory Rising, Furious Sound of Glory* and *Enthroned*

"'The wave's already here! The wave's already here! It just looks different!' were the words I heard the Lord say recently. It's so encouraging when the Lord confirms Himself through someone else. Jennifer Martin's *Awaken: The Dark Horse Prophet*, left me shaking my head in agreement! The Lord is calling out prophets from every nation, that carry purity in their actions and words, bear no completion or jealousy for one another, and truly want to see JESUS GET THE GLORY! Are you one of these God is calling out that will radically shift the prophetic movement?"

—ANA WERNER
Founder of Ana Werner Ministries, President of *Eagles Network*
Author of *The Seer's Path, Seeing Behind the Veil, The Warrior's Dance,* co-author of *Accessing the Greater Glory*
www.anawerner.org

"If there was ever a time to hear the heartbeat of God, it is now. He has been raising up friends of God, who would choose to hear his whispers over the crowd, and share his mysteries. Jennifer is one of those true friends of God. In the pages of this book you will be drawn into deeper intimacy with the King of Kings, as well as mobilized and commissioned for the greatest move of God we have ever seen on the earth. The dreams, visions, and throne-room insights in the pages of this book will have you hungrily peering through the veil with anticipation, and stir you deeply to be used in the days to come."

—CHRISTY JOHNSTON
Everyday Revivalists
Author of *Releasing Prophetic Solutions* & *Prophetic Voice*

"*Awaken: The Dark Horse Prophet* will awaken you from your slumber and chart a path, leading you out of the valley of hopelessness. While pounding the keys on her computer, Jennifer has created a magnum opus, a work of art that prophetically calls forth a company of dreamers to their place of destiny. You are never too young or too old to dream. If you keep believing, the dream that you wish will come true (Cinderella)."

—DON MILAM
Acquisitions Consultant, *Whitaker House*

To my husband, Munday, whose constant faith encourages me to believe in my calling and reach for more than I ever thought possible.

And to my children, Samuel, who teaches me to think deeper and never give up, and JennaBeth, who reminds me to look at the stars and dream. I pray that you will take the baton that Jesus hands to you and run with all your heart.

I love you.

CONTENTS

FOREWORD

What a brilliant book! It is so good that I wish I had written it. But I did not. Jennifer Martin of Contagious Love International did—and it is her first book. Well, it won't be her last—that's for sure. Why do I love this book? Well, let me share a few thoughts with you.

First of all, I know the author. I have been one of the prophetic papas in Munday and Jennifer Martin's life for the last several years. We live in the same greater region of Nashville, Tennessee. I have watched these two kids get married, travel the globe, raise a family, and take every step of the way quite well. I have watched Jennifer grow and emerge with her own distinct voice and anointing in the Holy Spirit.

Second, this is fresh revelation. I thought I knew what the content of this book was all about, until I read it. A Dark Horse?

A Dark Horse Prophet? A Dark Horse Movement? Dark Horse Minstrels? Huh? What is this lady talking about?!? What a dream she opens with—and the way Jennifer unpacks the symbolism is a great lesson in itself. It is a great example of revelation, interpretation and application. But where the revelation is personal and the approach to the interpretation is distinct, the empowerment into calling is also stunning. Simply, stunning!

Third, the writing style is captivating and distinct. Jennifer conveys truth that becomes so convincing, but yet done without being heavy handed. She takes you on a relational journey of learning how to walk with the Holy Spirit. She opens the door to the next chamber of understanding, while whetting your appetite to keep on reading, eating, and devouring what she has penned. One thought, another revelation, all which leads you to another nuance, another twist, another invitation to stop and pray and become what you are reading.

Fourth, this book, *Awaken: The Dark Horse Prophet*, is centered in Jesus and on the Word of God. Some next generation leaders today, who can flow smoothly in the river of the supernatural, tend to be wordless. Great stories and great experiences. But I am often left with the old statement, *"Where's the beef?"* Well, don't worry, this manuscript is filled with the Word of God, couched between dreams, prayers, exhortations, and passionate calls to grow up.

So, if you feel like you were born for something that has not yet come, and your heart aches for it, look no further. You are probably one of these dark horses in training! This book is written about you!

It is with great joy and honor that I commend to you the life, ministry, and now the writings of Jennifer Martin. Well done. The only thing wrong with this book is that it ends! I think I see a series coming on the Journey unto an Awakened Heart.

—JAMES W GOLL
GOD ENCOUNTERS MINISTRIES

AUTHOR'S NOTE

I chose to write the "Awaken" collection, with *The Dark Horse Prophet* being one of many, because I want to see the heart awakened in you and truth to blossom deeply within. I want you to capture a glimpse of my heart also that you may not otherwise obtain through my teachings. I am a dreamer. And this is the place where I want to share secret dreams given to me by God. They are intimate. They are impactful. And they are set apart for you. May this collection take you on a journey through the many streams of the Father's heart, and awaken the heart within you.

"He reveals deep and secret things; He knows what is in the darkness, And light dwells with Him." (Daniel 2:22)

INTRODUCTION

I sat on my tan sofa this past New Year's Eve, pondering in my heart what would take place this year. *What is God's plan, I wonder, for this year and the following decade?*

I thought I would take a chance and ask, "Father, will you show me what you are planning in the future?"

I didn't know what kind of answer, if any, I would receive, but a childlike heart is full of questions, isn't it? You know what they say, "it couldn't hurt to ask."

He answered me that night in a dream. But before I share the dream with you, I want to ask—do you believe God speaks through dreams to reveal secrets to us? I believe He does. Look at history.

Throughout the Scriptures, God speaks through dreams of things to come in the earth and in His Kingdom. He forewarned Pharaoh of the destruction coming to Egypt's crops and livestock when He bombarded him with dreams (Genesis 41). Thank God,

Pharaoh responded to the dream, and Joseph was there to interpret the meaning. Because God spoke and they listened, nations were saved from starvation and death.

Gideon heard about a dream that a man had and knew God was sending them a message of the victory He would give to Israel (Judges 7:13-15). Gideon was paying attention.

The Lord appeared to Solomon in a dream and said, *"Ask what you wish me to give you,"* (1 Kings 3:4-15). Wow, I would love God to say that to me! Wouldn't you?

The magi were *"warned by God in a dream not to return to Herod"* (Matthew 2:12). One dream protected the Savior from certain death before His time. Jesus was protected again from death in Matthew 2:13 (NIV), when the *"angel of the Lord appeared to Joseph in a dream. "Get up," he said, "take the child and his mother and escape to Egypt. Stay there until I tell you, for **Herod is going to search for the child to kill him."***

Luke tells us in Acts 16:9 that *"a vision appeared to Paul in the night: a man of Macedonia was standing and appealing to him, and saying, 'Come over to Macedonia and help us.'"* A vision in the night —yet again God used a dream to cause the gospel message to be brought to an unreached people.

These accounts are only a few of the many instances where God spoke in dreams or visions of the night. He spoke to believers, unbelievers, and leaders of nations through dreams. He still does today! I have had countless messages and warnings come to me in dreams. If I had not listened, I would have suffered.

I want you to listen to this dream with all of your heart. I pray your eyes are open to see, and your ears open to hear what the Holy Spirit is saying to the church and the world.

God is sending a powerful message through this dream. I know that as you soak it in you will be filled with fresh vision and passion for the part that you play in the Kingdom. This dream wasn't just for me. It's also for you.

1

DARK HORSES DREAM

I WAS in the middle of the ocean, with nothing around me. I held onto an inner tube with my right arm. My left arm was free. I'm not sure how I was able to hold on with one arm, because there was chaos in the water. I was surrounded by three waves. Each wave was positioned like the points on a triangle, and I was in the center. There was a wave in front of me, one behind me to my right and one behind me to my left. They all faced me in the center. Each wave had individual movement and continued to crest and break. Then the three waves moved together in a circular motion around me, forming a whirlpool. I realized that I was about to go on a crazy ride. I was either going to get sucked into this thing, or it was going to take me on the fastest carousel ride ever. I knew I had better hold on to that inner tube for dear life.

I looked to my left and I saw my son, Samuel, very close to me. The whirlpool was picking up speed and it was only a matter of time until he was hit by it. I knew I had to help him, because he didn't see the obvious waves that were churning in the waters. He didn't know his life was in the balance. So I reached out with my left hand and grabbed him, just as we entered the force of the spin at a high speed. Somehow the waves moved over us without affecting us. Thankfully, we were left unharmed.

Then it was just the two of us, alone, floating. The water stilled. Everything quieted. I felt so grateful that we had survived. I looked to my right towards the shore, and the waves that had passed us continued in the circular motion straight towards the beach. It moved the way a hurricane moves, spinning yet traveling forward in one direction.

Then I looked to my left. A huge wall of water, hundreds of feet high, was speeding toward us. There was no time to react. I knew it would take our lives within seconds. We could not make it through this. I remember screaming, "We have to get ashore right now!"

Just as I said this, we were transported to the shore immediately. One moment I was looking at the water about to overtake us, and the next I was standing on the beach. I watched this same wall of water as it neared the shoreline. The other waves had vanished, and this immeasurable wall was the only force moving in the waters. Then, like a waterfall from the top of a building, it became the most fearful and beautiful thing I'd ever seen. Just before it hit the shore it turned into the shape of horses, moving with great strength towards the land. It only lasted for a moment —the motion was so fluid. Then, it dissipated onto the sand.

The horses were gone. I was so sad when I realized they weren't real. I wanted so badly to see them emerge out of the waters and run with full force inland. What a sight that would have been!

Still on the beach, but farther inland now, my attention was drawn to my right where I saw total darkness. A dark and dry land stretched out as far as the eye could see. There was no grass, no life. What a drastic change from what I had just experienced.

Just then, as if a door in the ground opened, I looked and saw a dark brown horse emerge from below, as if coming up a ramp onto the land. Then another right behind it, and another, until before I knew it, an entire herd was running wild and fearless with full speed across the dry expanse. As their hooves made contact with the earth, the magnificence of that sound echoed and vibrated the atmosphere. Their momentum never slowed while they ran. I gazed in wonder.

One of the horses saw me and was drawn towards me. It made a beeline right towards me, as if I was its destiny. It galloped up to me, and I reached out my hand to pet its face right between the eyes. I slowly ran my hand down its nose. It was so worked up from the intensity of the racing herd that I feared it might be too wild. I had to soothe and calm it down to bring it peace.

Immediately, the horse changed into a cow. I noticed it had an open sore on its face, where it had gotten hurt escaping through a fence. I realized this cow was in labor and was going to give birth at any minute. Samuel was beside me, and he said he knew what to do. He jumped into position behind the cow while I continued stroking its face to keep it calm. I was worried that it would kick my son, not understanding that we were here to help. As Samuel began to assist the birth of the calf, just like a veterinarian, I woke up.

———

Now is that wild or what! Our God loves to reveal mysteries to us. Psalm 78:2 says, *"I will open my mouth in a parable: I will utter dark sayings of old."* And one of my favorite verses, Deuteronomy 29:29 tells us, *"The secret things belong unto the Lord our God, but the things **revealed** belong unto us and to our children forever, that we may follow all the words of this law."*

Let's open this riddle and go on a journey into God's heart together.

DECODING THE DREAM

I believe the ocean represents the nations and the three waves represent the three waves of outpouring in America in the last century. Samuel represents the prophets of God and also the next generation. I represent worship and intercession because that is the anointing on my life. The circular tube represents covenant and cycles. My right arm represents salvation and my left arm rescues the prophet of God, who didn't "see" the wave coming. We were caught up in the three waves of outpouring.

THE FIRST WAVE

The "First Wave" was the Pentecostal revival of the Holy Spirit in the early 1900s, beginning in Topeka, Kansas, in 1901 under the leadership of Charles Parham. In 1906 we saw the Azusa Street revival headed by William Seymour and Frank Bartleman. God moved in extraordinary power with miracles, healings, and the gifts of the Spirit, including speaking in tongues, as people were baptized in the Spirit. People came from all over the world to experience the power of God, in a small house on Bonnie Brae Street in Los Angeles, California. This was the catalyst for many others during that time. The anointing we see moving in the first wave is the outpouring of the Holy Spirit and the gifts of the Spirit in operation.

THE SECOND WAVE

The second wave was revival across denominations during the 60s and 70s. It followed the "Voice of Healing" movement during the mid-1940s to 50s, the outpouring of miracles and healing power to hundreds of thousands across the land, which we are going to see cycle back around in this next decade. It began with the Catholic Charismatic Renewal and spread throughout many other streams, birthing the Word of Faith movement and many more, including the Jesus People movement. The second wave has the anointing of the revelation of the Word of God and faith in Him.

THE THIRD WAVE

The third wave began with John Wimber and the Vineyard, bringing new sounds and a revolution to the worship scene in the 1980s and 1990s. This led into the Father's Blessing in Toronto, which catapulted a worldwide awakening. The anointing we see that came forth in the third wave is the sound of heaven, the new song, and high praise.

So, Samuel (the prophet) and I (worship and intercession) represent some of those in the prophetic worship and prayer movement who have been caught up in asking for these waves of God to come again, but not "seeing" what is coming on the horizon right now, the Fourth Wave. For those who have ears to hear, let them hear what the Spirit is saying to the Church. And those that have eyes to see, let them see.

We, as people of God, have been so caught up in these waves, in the whirlpool of these waves, even prophesying that another wave is coming like these, that we don't recognize the new wave God is sending. I don't want to miss it. Do you?

Don't get me wrong. I honor every wave of God and study it, because I'm hungry for however He wants to move. We love to say, "Do it again, God." Samuel and I were riding in those three waves. And the people of God are still riding those waves today. God was showing me that we've been stuck in these three waves —we've been riding them, we've been looking at them, we've been waiting for the next wave to look like these three waves. Or even just one of them. We honor them. But we are not going to see the same kind of movement come forth that we've seen before. God is doing a new thing. He has another wave coming that we didn't expect. Many don't see it coming. And many don't know that it's already here. We need to get ready now!

Let's pause here for a minute, because I want to share with you what I heard the Lord say recently. There were dreams that led up to the Dark Horse Dream.

2

THE BOWLS ARE TIPPED

I HEARD IT LOUD, so very loud in my spirit while driving home in the pouring rain. Without hesitation, I began to decree, "The bowls are tipped!" The prayers of the saints have filled the bowls for decades and they have reached their tipping point. Now the prayers are continually coming and causing a massive overflow of the bowls. Now is the time for the answers to speedily pour forth onto the earth. And a great harvest of souls is here. It's not the time to stop or slow down, but we must continually come to the Lord and overflow the bowls. *The outpouring of prayers is causing the heavens to give rain and the earth is bringing forth her precious fruit to her God: Souls! Souls! Souls!*

DREAM ABOUT THE GOLDEN BOWLS

I dreamed I was standing before a large beast that stood like a man on two legs and had fur all over its body, with two horns on its head. I was unafraid of this beastly looking man, because I had a weapon. I picked up my leather sling, just like David's, and I placed a golden bowl at the end of it. I began to swing the sling around as I stepped forward towards the beast. I hit him in the head, over and over again. He was rendered powerless, unable to attack me, unable to move, because the golden bowl had paralyzed him!

THE GOLDEN BOWLS

Have you heard of these golden bowls? They are found in the book of Revelation. These are the bowls that the twenty-four elders hold in one hand, while holding a harp in the other. They are filled with incense and are the prayers of the saints (Rev. 5:8). God loves prayers, obviously, as he refers to them as being incense. Remember when Cornelius was visited by the angel who told him, "Your prayers and alms have ascended as a memorial before God" (Acts 10:4). God could smell the aroma coming up before Him.

Your prayers smell sweet to Him! How long before the sweetness of your heartfelt prayers overwhelms the atmosphere of Heaven, and their incense is smelled by all? There must be a tipping point. There must be a fullness of time when those prayers are answered. I believe the time is now! The collective prayers of the saints have filled the air of Heaven. God smells it every second! The angels smell it constantly. Let the incense rise! Let it fill Heaven! Let it cause God's heart to be moved with compassion and send the rain.

Zechariah 10:1 (NKJV) tells us to *"Ask the Lord for rain, in the time of the latter rain."* God wants us to ask, and He gives the invitation: *"Ask, and it will be given to you; seek, and you will find; knock, and it will be opened to you. For everyone who asks receives, and he who seeks finds, and to him who knocks it will be opened."* (Matt. 7:7). Let the Spirit and the Bride say, "Come!" He desires to pour out, but he waits to be asked. The Church has been asking and asking, seeking and seeking, knocking and knocking, and I hear the Lord saying, "The incense of your prayers has come continually before Me. I have heard you." He is sending the rain, and he is sending it now!

THE RAIN FOR THE HARVEST

He is pouring out his Spirit and he is reaping a great harvest of souls unto himself, and it is now! On May 5, 2017, I had a dream. The number five represents grace, so 5/5 (May 5) is double grace. I was standing in a field of worshippers and each had an umbrella, but it was not raining. They were pouring out their heart before God in the most beautiful, deep love I had ever felt, yet without making one sound. It was completely quiet, and very holy. I could feel their hearts wide open to Jesus. Then suddenly (get ready for a suddenly), it began to downpour the heaviest rain. I couldn't see the people anymore—all I could see was rain!

In the dream, the Spirit of God came upon me and I prophesied, "This rain is a sign that God has heard us! He is sending revival to America!"

The next day I looked for weather patterns that might confirm the dream. I knew that God likes to confirm his Word. Sure enough, I found that the days leading up to that dream had been a historic week of flooding. It was breaking records across many states—this rain is a sign. Now I knew that the dream was on time.

After that, in the next scene in the dream, God took me to a place where I was speaking to those who had laid down their lives for intercession, the ones who have believed God and have been filling the prayer bowls of Heaven for decades. I prophesied to them: "You will have a part in the reaping of this harvest!"

Prayer warriors, you will have a part in it. Your labor has not been in vain. Hear me, the fruit of your prayers is here. You will see it! This is to encourage the intercessors and prayer warriors across this nation that God has heard you!

In the final part of the dream, I was walking with my father and a great friend of mine, Charlie Shamp, who is a revivalist and powerful evangelist to the world. We were talking about the revival coming. We walked together, my dad on my right side and my friend on the left. We stopped at a round garden, filled with very large, ripe strawberries. I knew this represented healing and intimate love, because strawberries are known as the romance fruit. Romans 5:5 tells us *"the love of God has been poured out within our hearts through the Holy Spirit."* This love will spark the flame of true worship. ***This revival will be full of intimacy and healing of the nations!*** I could feel the expectancy of this outpouring and the joy of God.

My dad represents the generation of intercessors who have given their lives for this in prayer, as he has done himself. My evangelist friend, Charlie, represents those that will go into the whole world to reap the great harvest. And we walked together.

Did you hear that? *We walked together.*

Intercessors and evangelists must come together in the Spirit. We must walk together. True worship, like in the beginning of the dream, added to decades of intercession and the power of the evangelistic movement, will usher in the greatest awakening and the largest youth revival this world has ever seen. It's coming. It's here!

THE WAVE IS HERE

Bob Jones, a prophet of God, prophesied that the year 2020 would mark the beginning of the billion soul youth harvest. It would be the harvest of harvesters. Bob Jones went to be with the Lord on Valentine's Day, 2-14, 2014. There's a sign in itself. God is love. His words that He gave to Bob were because of His great love for the world. And what Bob Jones prophesied is coming to pass now. Stadiums are being filled with young hungry people and they want purity and holiness. They want to see God. The Bible says, *"Blessed are the pure in heart, for they shall see God" (Matthew 5:8).*

I want to share another recent dream. I was on a shoreline and people were asking me, "When do you think the wave is coming?" They had heard of a wave, but were unsure of its arrival time. I looked out to sea, and to my right was a wave as tall as the sky. Unafraid, I looked back at the people and said, "The wave is already here."

Did you hear that? The wave isn't coming. It's already here!

The biggest wave is here! It's the fourth wave. I saw it back in that dream and then again in the dark horse dream. It's a convergence of the three waves that have gone before us, just as the waves passed Samuel and me in the water. These waves have come and gone. God is moving His children out of the place of looking to the outpourings of the past, causing their attention to look to the new. He's going to cause their faces to turn, just like my face turned to see the wave. They will hear the Word of the Lord, and see exactly what he is doing. They will discern that, truly, another wave is on its way. It's bigger, and it has an entirely different flow. The true prophets of God will see it. Amos 3:7 says, "surely the Lord GOD does nothing, unless He reveals His secret to His servants the prophets." They will see this movement, and they will prophesy about it. It may have a different language or presentation, but it's the same message—"the Fourth Wave is here."

And, I saw this fourth wave, as a wave of dark horses.

3

THE FOURTH WAVE OF THE DARK HORSES

THE WAVE TURNED into a wall of rushing waters, with the appearance of horses galloping towards the shore. They were dark-colored horses.

A dark horse is "a little-known person or thing that emerges to prominence." You've probably heard this phrase used to refer to someone unexpectedly winning a competition or race. A dark horse in a horse race would come out of nowhere to win. All odds are against it. But somehow it takes the trophy, making every jaw in the place drop. A totally unexpected turn of events.

So, "Who are these dark horses," you ask. Well, in the dream, I saw them come forth from the ocean, which represents the many nations of the earth. Then, I saw them crash ashore, because that's how it will be. They will crash upon us all, suddenly arriving and quickly arising. And they will proceed to rise up out of every nation, as I saw them arise from the dry earth.

The dark horses are many that God is raising up in this hour.

We won't see them coming. They have been hidden in the earth. They're coming from every tribe and from every tongue. They will come out of the nations and crash ashore. We will hear them referred to as "dark horses." Even candidates for political offices are coming forth that nobody saw coming. Just as I saw them emerge from the barren, dry land, some will rise out of the dust, out of the dry spiritual nations, where there is no water. People will say, "How could one rise out of that nation?" like they said about Jesus coming out of Nazareth. Others will rise out of their dry spiritual lives, where they have been thirsty for God. They will awaken and rise to their rightful place as sons and daughters of God. They will awaken to the calling on their life, and they will run. They have sought the Lord in prayer, in the secret place, and have obeyed His voice. They have waited. And their time has come.

> *"But those who wait on the LORD shall renew their strength; they shall mount up with wings like eagles; they shall run, and not be weary; they shall walk, and not faint"* (Isaiah 40:31 NKJV).

The dark horses shall arise and cause a shift in the prophetic movement. Suddenly, there will be prominent prophetic voices releasing the word of the Lord with on-time words and pinpoint accuracy. These words will cause a turning of hearts. The Bible says the spirit of Elijah would come before the coming of the Lord.

> *"And he will turn the hearts of the fathers to the children, And the hearts of the children to their fathers"* (Malachi 4:6 NKJV).

They are coming out of the darkness into the Light.

"For, behold, the darkness will cover the earth, and deep darkness the peoples: but the LORD will rise upon you, and his glory will appear upon you" (Isaiah 60:2).

People are going to say, "Who are these people? Where did they come from?" They're going to ask questions. The answer is, "They are the dark horses of God, who have been hidden but are now going to be revealed, for such a time as this."

God led me to this verse, and it confirms this dream. Look what it says!

"For they will draw out the abundance of the seas, and the hidden treasures of the sand" (Deuteronomy 33:19).

Isn't that amazing?

I saw the abundance of horses coming from the sea, and out of the sand. They are treasures to God and to the world. And we shall partake of the treasures they bring. Let us receive them.

These dark horses will preach the Gospel, heal the sick, cleanse the lepers, and raise the dead. They'll give living water to the dying. They will carry the three waves closely knitted within their hearts, and become the fourth wave, which is the anointing of the previous three waves moving as one. Like a threefold cord is not easily broken (Ecclesiastes 4:12).

MOVING IN THE POWER OF THE HOLY SPIRIT (FIRST WAVE)

They are going to move with the Holy Spirit—in tune with

him. They will yield to the Holy Spirit and say, "What are you saying, God? How are you moving?" They won't resist him, because they fear him with all their hearts, and even deeper than that, because they love him. Many miracles and signs will follow them. They are going to walk in extreme authority and power. They're going to know it in confidence, but with great humility. Their hearts are pure before God. What God has spoken to them will come upon them and cause them to shine forth his majesty to the nations.

FULL OF THE WORD OF GOD AND FAITH (SECOND WAVE)

They're going to be full of the Word of God, loving Scripture and talking about it with others. Carrying a full knowledge of the Word of God, they will speak the truth of the Kingdom of God and his majesty to the nations. They will not be afraid to call people out of their dark sin and into the Light, *releasing the Word of the Lord Jesus Christ and reaping a great harvest of souls, for the Kingdom of heaven is at hand!*

RELEASING TRUE WORSHIP (THIRD WAVE)

They're going to be true worshippers like the third wave, the Vineyard movement, that released a fresh sound of intimate praise and celebration. The true worshippers are going to bring forth this new high praise to God. It's a sound of power and authority that comes from a place of knowing who their King is. Some of these dark horses are the next worship leaders, bringing us into the new praise and worship movement. There will be fresh sounds in the congregations. The dark horse minstrels are arising. They don't bow to the traditions of man. They change the atmosphere. They offer the complete sound of high praise to their King.

Does This Sound Like You? Are You a Dark Horse?

This might be you. Maybe you didn't think that you were one of them. God is going to have a horse trot right up to you and look you straight in the eyes. You will sense that you are one of the dark horses, and you are going to prophesy the Word of the Lord. And you are going to receive the other dark horses who are called forth. No competition. No jealousy. One body together in the harvest of souls for the glory of Jesus Christ. God is raising up his dark horses in every area of culture and in every sphere of influence. What is your sphere of influence? What are you crying out for? And more importantly, *who* are you crying out for?

God hears your voice, crying out in the wilderness of your life. First, he wants you to be refreshed and come out of the desolate spiritual desert. Maybe you've been spiritually thirsty, and you felt dry. God is going to cause a rebirthing in you. He's going to cause you to drink again of his living water that flows from his throne. And Jesus is the Shepherd who will lead you there. , *"For the Lamb who is in the midst of the throne will shepherd them and lead them to living fountains of waters. And God will wipe away every tear from their eyes."* (Revelation 7:17 NKJV)

You will be refreshed and reignited to run the race set before you. He's going to cause you to come forth. He's going to wake you up in your heart. He's going to awaken your hearing, and you are going to prophesy the Word of the Lord. Do you believe that God wants to use you? Jesus said, *"If you believe, you will see the glory of God"* (John 11:40). God is activating in you this year your destiny, your purpose, and who you are in him. You're going to come into a place where the power of God overtakes you, and you become intertwined with the Holy Spirit—walking with him, talking with him, seeing what he's doing, and hearing what he's saying.

Then, you're going to take everything you receive from him and release it to people everywhere you go, especially out in public, without any agenda, just proclaiming the Good News. Jesus wasn't looking for a platform or a position in the church. He wasn't looking to be the one in the spotlight. He was in the streets, every day, looking for the will of God, looking for a lost people, looking for the broken—people who needed miracles or healing. He was always in search of the captive, so that he might set them free. Jesus said, *"The Spirit of the Lord is upon me, because he has anointed me to preach the gospel to the poor; he has sent me to heal the brokenhearted, to preach deliverance to the captives, and recovering of sight to the blind, to set at liberty them that are bruised"* (Luke 4:18 NKJV). He loved being out in the streets. He desired to be with the ones he loved, the ones his Father loved. Jesus was a dark horse. And no one saw him coming.

You are one of the dark horses called forth in this season to run this race set before you. Whether called to leadership in the larger body or simply in your family, it doesn't matter, as long as you are obeying the words of Jesus and letting his Kingdom flow into your life and to the lives of those around you.

WHAT ABOUT THE COW?

The dark horse turned into a cow. I thought, "Lord, why would you turn a horse into a cow?" I thought of the saying "cash cow," representing wealth. A cow represents the abundant provision of God. The Bible says in Psalm 50:10 that he owns *the cattle on a thousand hills."* And in Deuteronomy 28:4 (NKJV) we are promised, *"Blessed shall be the fruit of your body, the produce of your ground and the increase of your herds, the increase of your cattle and the offspring of your flocks."* So the dark horse that turned into a cow is the symbolic meaning of the ones who will carry and birth the wealth and provision needed for the Kingdom of God. I believe it's not only natural provision, but also spiritual wealth, which is far better than gold. I believe we will see this birthing release a blessing over the land. Listen to what this verse says,

> *"Then you shall see and become radiant, and your heart shall swell with joy; because the abundance of the sea shall be turned to you, the wealth of the Gentiles shall come to you"* (Isaiah 60:5 NKJV).

The sea shall be turned to you. The three waves turned towards me and moved around me. The abundance of the sea represents nations, but it also means riches or wealth. Here we see God giving us another hidden meaning of the wealth being turned to us, the Body of Christ.

I don't know what it's going to look like. I don't know how it's going to sound. But I know that prosperity will come forth when these dark horses are released.

THE WOUNDED WARRIORS

The cow was fenced in, but it broke loose. It was wounded as it tried to break free. This will be the case for these dark horses. *They will break free of the places they were bound.* They will fight the system, and some will be rejected and wounded by others. Some will come out of great darkness, having to break the power of sin in their lives. They may bear many wounds and scars, but their hearts will be pure. And what they bring forth will cause wealth and blessing to spring up among the nations of the earth.

When the wounds are healed and these warriors realize who they are *in Christ,* and they begin to walk as the sons and daughters of God on the earth, it is going to release a supernatural blessing over the land. There is going to be an increase of wealth among the nations. The abundance of the seas shall come to us. There is going to be a huge release. *"For the anxious longing of the creation waits eagerly for the revealing of the sons of God. For we know that the whole creation groans and suffers the pains of childbirth together until now."* (Romans 8:19, 22). The earth is moaning and groaning for the release of these sons and daughters to come into their rightful inheritance as heirs of the Kingdom.

The Spirit of God has been waiting for the Bride to rise and take her place beside her King. The Church is waking up. We know that this is the season of awakening. We're here. We've known that for years. The Church has been in the preparation phase to get ready to stand beside her King. It's time.

HELP BIRTH THE PROMISE

This is all about to break loose! But this cow, this dark horse that became the promise of wealth and blessing, needs help birthing the promise. Just as I watched my son, Samuel, who represents the intercessors and prophets of God, who didn't "see" the waves coming, who began to aid the cow in giving birth because he "knew what to do," so too will prophets, intercessors, and the children of God awaken to discern the times. God is calling the intercessors and prophets to assist in the birthing by watching over this Word, with the Lord, to see it manifest through prayer. Their hearts will be turned towards the dark horses, and they will come alongside them as a new thing is birthed into the earth.

We must help birth the promise, people of God. I was stroking the nose of the horse, and then a cow, to keep it calm during the birthing process. I represent the intercessors and true worshippers that worship the Lord in spirit and in truth. You intercede prophetically in the spirit realm, and he's calling you to receive these dark horses and be there to bring peace to them. Peace is an absolute requirement of all those who desire to see birthing during this season. If you have ever been in a birthing room, then you know that the nurses are always calming the one in labor. This is their job. They know it is so important for the health of all involved, especially the mother and baby. So, intercessors and worshippers, you must be peacemakers in the Spirit. Jesus said, *"Blessed are the peacemakers: for they shall be called sons of God."* (Matt 5:9).

The prophets are responsible for birthing the promises of God. This is their job. They are to speak the decrees that God gives them. It's especially important that they speak into the lives of these dark horses and help them birth their callings. They must be ever present and ready to assist those God brings to their care. They will recommend them and support them. Because of this, great blessing will come to the Body of Christ and the entire earth will reap the rewards. It's time to lay down our lives for our friends, like Jesus asks us, and show the greatest love of all.

Let's not let jealousy, contentions, and strife come in with every evil work and bring division into this work of the Holy Spirit. The enemy will try to sow tares amongst the wheat and drain the life from the Body of Christ. We must be alert.

We must become that three-stranded cord that moves as one, not easily broken—the dark horses, intercessors, and the prophets. Three strands, but one mighty cord. We need to stand with them, hand in hand—for them, not against them.

There's a great story Jesus told in Matthew 20:1-16,

For the kingdom of heaven is like a landowner who went out early in the morning to hire laborers for his vineyard. When he had agreed with the laborers for a denarius for the day, he sent them into his vineyard. And he went out about the third hour and saw others standing idle in the market place; and to those he said, 'You also go into the vineyard, and whatever is right I will give you.' And so they went. Again he went out about the sixth and the ninth hour, and did the same thing. And about the eleventh hour he went out and found others standing around; and he *said to them, 'Why have you been standing here idle all day long?' They *said to him, 'Because no one hired us.' He *said to them, 'You go into the vineyard too.'

"When evening came, the owner of the vineyard *said to his foreman, 'Call the laborers and pay them their wages, beginning with the last group to the first.' When those hired about the eleventh hour came, each one received a denarius. When those hired first came, they thought that they would receive more; but each of them also received a denarius. When they received it, they grumbled at the landowner, saying, 'These last men have worked only one hour, and you have made them equal to us who have borne the burden

and the scorching heat of the day.' But he answered and said to one of them, 'Friend, I am doing you no wrong; did you not agree with me for a denarius? Take what is yours and go, but I wish to give to this last man the same as to you. Is it not lawful for me to do what I wish with what is my own? Or is your eye envious because I am generous?' So the last shall be first, and the first last.

Let's not be like the ones who grumbled at the end of the day because they received the same wages as those who arrived late. They got so upset because they worked longer and harder, thinking they were due more reward, right? Some of you prophetic intercessors have been praying and asking God to move in a fresh outpouring again for many, many years. Now God is asking you to receive the ones who are coming straight out of darkness and into the harvest fields. They will only live for evangelism. They will be "too wild," "too radical," and take it "too far." All they want to do is go out and find the lost treasures of the earth. This is going to be one of the main thrusts of their message. They're going to awaken the heart, and awaken the Church to reach the lost for Jesus Christ.

We must come together and not let the enemy bring division and devour what God has planted. It is our duty to follow the words of Jesus and let the fruit of His Spirit work in us. Let us serve one another in love. The greatest commandment is, *'You shall love the Lord your God with all your heart, and with all your soul, and with all your mind.' The second is like it: 'You shall love your neighbor as yourself.'* (Matthew 22: 37,39).

The dark horses of God are going to pioneer a new movement, and they're going to birth forth something in the earth that has been long-awaited for. They're going to burn for God and his government on the earth that will have no end. I believe it's the season of the coming of the Lord. I believe we are getting ready for the Lord right now. It could be many years away, but we are here, preparing the way of the Lord. And those who receive these dark horses, and get in line with heaven's plans, are going to receive a great reward. But if you are like me, you only care about one reward, hearing those beautiful words from Jesus, *'Well done, good and faithful servant; you have been faithful over a few things, I will make you ruler over many things. Enter into the joy of your lord.'* (Matthew 25:23 NKJV).

It's time to start receiving the whole body of Christ. Let's work together in unity and community. God is no respecter of persons. There are no "big I's and little u's." It's time for all of us to come together and support one another, like a team does when they play a game. One person doesn't try to get all the glory. The whole team wants to get all the glory. This is a great picture of how to win this race. We work together. Let every member play his or her part.

Many of the dark horses are already around you. Some might be in your congregation. Some may be in your family or in your neighborhood. You need to start pouring into them. They may not look like the normal prophets or intercessors, or sound like normal worship leaders, but God knows what treasure lies within them. We want to receive the voice of the Lord, but we sometimes miss the package it comes in. Let's not miss it, friends.

God has many colors in the wind of the Spirit. We must receive and celebrate the uniqueness in each one of us. Don't compare yourself and think, "Well, I don't look like anybody else. I don't feel like anybody else. I must not be anointed or chosen by God." If I try to sound like somebody else, or look like somebody else, I wouldn't be myself, and it wouldn't be authentic. It wouldn't be real. God wouldn't want it, because he loves me. God wants truth in the inward parts. He longs to hear my heart. He wants to feel my heartbeat. He has uniquely and wonderfully made each and every one of us (Psalm 139:14). That's what it's all about.

The dark horses are going to bring people back into this awakening—of knowing that it's all about union with Christ. It's all for the One. We need to truly know who we are in Christ and our identity, so that we can call forth destiny in these dark horses who are rising up. Maybe they don't even know it yet, but you see the calling on their life. You know how important it is when you have someone around to see your gifts, to encourage you to press on towards the mark of the high calling in Christ Jesus. They need us to begin to call forth their gifts to manifest in the earth.

ISRAEL'S PROMISE

While this word is for all nations, God spoke to me that this dream has a major connection to Israel and America. Specifically, there is a promise for Israel coming forth.

In Isaiah 66:8 (NKJV) it says, *"shall a nation be born at once? For as soon as Zion was in labor, She gave birth to her children."* Zion is referring to the nation of Israel. The promise to Israel begins in Isaiah 60 and goes all the way through Chapter 66. I would encourage you to go read the entire section for yourself. Ask the Holy Spirit to show you if we might be in this time now. I'm going to be bold and say I believe we're in the prophetic fulfillment of those Scriptures. Israel is waiting for her Messiah. She's waiting for the second coming of the Lord, which is at hand.

Isaiah 60 says that all the wealth of the Gentiles shall come into Israel, and that the Gentiles will come from every nation and walk in her streets. Her gates will not be closed day or night. Is this not exactly what is happening right now in Israel? We are seeing these Scriptures come to life in our time. We need to be awake and look. This is happening now. Isaiah 66 talks about labor and birthing of a nation. I believe the dark horses are also going to come forth out of Israel. All of this is going to tie in together, because as Israel is blessed and we support Israel, the world will be blessed. God loves Israel. The Bible says to *"Rejoice with Jerusalem, and be glad with her, all you that love her"* (Isaiah 66:10 NKJV).

Isaiah 60:5 (NKJV) tells Israel, *"Then you shall see and become radiant, and your heart shall swell with joy; because the abundance of the sea shall be turned to you, the wealth of the Gentiles shall come to you."*

So here we see the seas and wealth correlation again. There is a promise for Israel. Pray for Israel. Rejoice with her. Prophetic fulfillment is at hand. We need to recognize the season we are in. *It's here. It's really, really here!*

Interesting fact: America leads the world in horse population at ten million plus, with the second highest nation having only six million. Could this be confirmation of the dream being a promise to America and all nations, as well as Israel? I believe so. Get ready. The fourth wave of the dark horses is here.

I received this dream as an answer to my question. "Father, would you give me a dream and tell me what you're doing this year in the Church and in the earth?" I asked him on January 1st, and that night He gave me this dream as the answer to my question.

Now God is issuing a decree throughout the earth. He is calling all dark horses to come forth.

First, you must hear and obey the call.

4

RENEWAL OF THE PROPHETIC

HAVE YOU BEEN CALLED? What has God called you to do? What dream has God been building within you? Some are called to be apostles, pastors, evangelists, teachers, and prophets. Many are called to these offices in the Spirit. Are you one of these? Or maybe you are called to the creative arts or media. There are many other spheres of influence. God is calling His children into every one of them. What sphere of influence has He given to you? Maybe it's a company, a job, a people group, or your family. How are you reaching out to others? What does your heart burn for? This is usually what you are called to do.

Some of you have burned in your hearts to release God's Word to the Body of Christ, and God has called you to be a prophet to the nations. God is raising up prophets who will speak his truth. They are not afraid of rejection or persecution. They are one part of the dark horse company. There is a renewal happening right now in the Spirit, bringing these truth givers forth. It's the renewal of the prophetic voice in the earth.

God has been preparing our hearts and building towards the release of the new company of dark horse prophets. I want to share a series of dreams I had in May of 2018, which lay a foundation for the call that has come forth in the Spirit.

WHO'S WATCHING THE BABY?

In a dream, I had just delivered a baby. I was nursing, and it was thriving. I was taking great care of the baby, and all was well. Then the scene changed, and the baby was about two years older. I knew that the baby was healthy, and I had done a good job taking care of it. Because I had been so faithful to watch over it, I became more relaxed. I knew I had friends around, and they would help me look after my baby, right? I thought to myself, "Oh, the baby's fine. I've got friends around. They love my baby. They'll take care of it. So I don't have to keep my eye on it every second. My child will be fine."

Then, suddenly, I realized that my child was nowhere around. Yet, all my friends were there. All the people I knew were there. I asked them, "Where is my baby? Where is my child? Are you guys not watching out for my child?"

They replied, "We don't know."

I went over to a pool and looked down into the water. There was the child at the bottom of the pool. It seemed to be alive, but probably not for too much longer. It would have drowned.

I woke up from that dream and asked the Lord, "What are you saying?"

I felt him say in my heart, "You need to watch over and care for your 'baby' that you have birthed."

What you have believed for, what God has spoken to your heart, is your "baby," and needs to be guarded and protected. Every believer is being called to the frontlines of God's army to watch over His Word and see it performed in their lives and their nation.

Leaders worldwide are being awakened. We're seeing calls to prayer. We're seeing calls to evangelism. We're seeing calls to fasting. We're seeing major hunger for God, across denominations, especially among the youth.

The baby has been birthed through prayer, the promise has arrived, but it must be protected through continual prayer and fasting. Maybe you've been nursing the promise and gotten to a place where everything was fine. You let down your guard just a bit.

We can't turn our back from our child. We can't assume that other people are going to watch our child for us. We can't even assume that heaven's going to watch our child for us.

It's not enough to say, "I've got the angels. I've got God. I've got the Holy Spirit. So everything will just be fine. I prayed already, so I don't need to keep praying."

Jesus said, "Ask, and keep on asking. Seek, and keep on seeking. Knock, and keep on knocking. For whoever asks, receives; whoever seeks, finds; and whoever knocks, the door will be opened."

You have an invitation to come into agreement with the Word of God and decree a release in the earth. We have to walk in agreement with what God is saying and not get lazy and complacent.

"Let us not become weary in doing good, for at the proper time we will reap a harvest if we do not give up" (Galatians 6:9 NIV).

Did you hear that? We will reap, IF we do not give up.

But that's when the enemy will try to find a way in, in weariness, and in the time of waiting, when we feel like giving up. Don't let him steal what God has rightfully given to you. It's your calling. It's your inheritance. Stay in one accord with heaven, pray and agree with what the Word of God says. Don't let tiredness rob you of what God has for you. Wait on God. Let's stay in agreement with heaven, and release the Word of the Lord. Let's guard our precious baby with all of our hearts.

There is a movement happening right now. The winds have changed. A new thing has come. Jesus said that we can look at the leaves of the trees and know when winter is near. So it is with the Spirit. I hear the Holy Spirit saying, "These are vital times we are living in. Everything is shifting towards a new wave."

I want to challenge you—even if you're at a place of breakthrough, and your prayers have been answered, it's not the time to sit back and say, "All is well, my breakthrough has come." We must remain alert and watch over our rightful inheritance through prayer.

I believe these next dreams confirm this even more.

THE RENEWAL OF THE PROPHETIC VOICE

The morning of Memorial Day, I woke up from another dream. I was at a service, where my husband, Munday Martin, was going to preach. I wanted to share something before he ministered. For some reason I stepped outside, and a group of people followed me. I knew they were ones that loved my ministry. I felt very close to them. There were about thirty of us, and I believe they were my Awaken The Heart people. *(Awaken The Heart is a live prayer, teaching, and prophesy video hour I started after God spoke to me in a dream. Go to www.ContagiousLove-Intl.com for more information)*

I turned around and said, "I don't want you to just come into this service and go home, like you just had another good service and nothing changed in your life. I don't want you to come into another meeting and have nothing affect you, nothing activated in you. I want you to experience real change. I want you to have real fruit in your life."

We went back into the service and sat down. Then I got up to deliver a Word of the Lord. I put on reading glasses, which is interesting, because I don't have reading glasses. Just as I was about to speak my friend, Charlie Shamp, jumps up. He had come to the meeting to support Munday and me. The Word of the Lord came on him to go and prophesy to somebody in the audience.

He went over to this person and he said, "Renewal, renewal, renewal, renewal, renewal!" over and over and over again.

Then the dream shifted, and I was in another dream. Have you ever awakened from a dream, but you were still dreaming, and *then* you woke up for real? This was one of those dreams—a dream within a dream. It's like layers upon layers, while you're dreaming.

I believe the Lord does this so that we really pay attention to what happens in the dream.

I woke up from the first dream, within another dream, and

I'm thinking about the dream that I just had. Somehow I'm talking to Charlie Shamp and telling him about this dream I just had with him in it.

Then, I began to prophesy to him, "The Lord is about to bring a renewal to the prophetic office. The Lord is about to bring a renewal to the prophetic voice." Then I woke up for real.

I knew to pay attention to both of these dreams. I went outside the church, because God is going to do something outside of what we think, outside of what we are used to, outside of the structure, outside of our mentality, outside of our pre-programmed notions of how God is going to move. The way he may move in your life may not be the way you expect. There's something else that's going to happen. It's not going to be a generic word that has no impact.

It is going to activate change in someone's life and take them where they need to go. I put on my glasses to get clear vision, and the Word comes forth. "Renewal!"

You may not know who Charlie Shamp is. God has called him to the office of a prophet for this generation, and he has been true to that office, with many detailed prophecies coming to pass for worldwide events. He represents renewal and the voice of the prophet. There is a renewal happening in the prophetic voice right now. The true prophets are arising, and they are going to speak the Word of the Lord.

As I shared these dreams with Munday, my favorite preacher by the way, he said, "Jennifer, it's also the prophetic voice of dreams. The Lord is restoring and renewing the prophetic voice through dream language." The voice of the dream interpreters is going to be heard on a new level. The dream interpreters, like

Joseph (see Genesis 41), will have favor with God and kings of nations.

We come into agreement with heaven. We're going to see that happen in your life.

THE OIL OF JOY

I had another dream only days later. It's my favorite part, with all of this coming together.

The Lord showed me a huge meeting where I was ministering. There were thousands of people, in every age group, but I remember noticing a lot of young people. As I ministered, I flowed, like the anointing on Kathryn Kuhlman, who was called by God as a young teen and saw powerful miracles and healings in large services throughout America back in the 1940s to 1970s. She would move with grace and eloquence across the stage, as her flowing white gown would sway when she walked. She said the Holy Spirit was her best friend and all she had. She moved very intimately with the voice of God, weeping, worshipping, and speaking truth as she called people to Jesus. People said the Presence of God was so strong that it was like thick electricity in the air.

I was ministering in this power of the Holy Spirit. I would lay hands on people and say, "The power of the Holy Spirit goes through this body right now." Maybe you've heard Kathryn say that, if you've ever listened to her.

I prayed for each person. As I did, the Holy Spirit touched them, but then a different wave came through after that. The power of the Holy Spirit knocked them down, and the presence of God came on me so strong that I couldn't stand. I literally had to drop to my hands and knees, and I had to crawl down the prayer line under the heavy presence of God.

This happened in the Bible. It says, *"that the priests could not stand to minister because of the cloud, for the glory of the LORD filled the house of the LORD."* (1 Kings 8:11).

The weight of his glory had come! I feel the Lord is saying right now that the weight of his glory is coming again to the Church. We are in this time of awakening. We're in this time of the fourth wave.

In my dream, I wanted people to have what God was releasing on me so badly that I literally crawled to each person who was standing in the line for prayer. I put my hands on their legs, because I couldn't reach any higher. I crawled by and touched their legs, and as I did, they fell out in the joy of the Holy Spirit, laughing. As I prayed for them, it came back on to me even stronger, and I would fall over again. I remember praying for the grace to be able to pray for every person, because *I* was so hungry for them to have what I was experiencing.

I don't want this only for myself. I want it for you, my friends. I care about you! I have a pastoral heart, which God has put in me. I have a prophetic pastoral gifting, and the Lord is giving me prophetic words and dreams that will help you pass through into your destiny. They will direct you where you need to go.

There is a joy of the Lord coming back to the Church, like we haven't seen in a while. It's like the Father's blessing of Toronto in 1994, which was notorious for the Presence of the Holy Spirit sparking laughter, healings, and praise. People came from all over the world to receive miracles, healings, and deliverance. Many testimonies came forth as people reported that their marriages were healed, cancers disappeared, and every type of healing imaginable was taking place. Laughter and joy filled the place where they gathered nightly as God swept through the room. We're going to see that release again. It will be like the Brownsville Revival in Pensacola, Florida, that exploded soon after the Toronto blessing on Father's Day, 1995. Evangelist Steve Hill was scheduled to share and the Holy Spirit poured out such conviction of sin in the people that they filled the altar to be saved. Nightly meetings began as Brother Steve stayed on as part of the revival.

It was packed every night and the power of God was so tangible.

People wanted to be baptized and the waters were so full of power that when people came up out of them their bodies would begin to shake with the power of God. This happened quite often to many.

It was a revival of the heart, calling people to wake up out of their sin and come to Jesus. They saw a lot of the joy of the Lord too, but they had a lot of repentance and fear of the Lord. They also had a lot of celebration and praise. The people wanted to let everything go and yield their lives to the Holy Spirit. They wanted to give their hearts to Jesus—completely and wholly surrendered.

Now we have these two outpourings, on the opposite sides of America, happening at the same time. And I heard the Lord tell me that this is going to release again in this fourth wave. We are going to see the fear of the Lord and true repentance touch people's hearts, with people weeping at the altars, truly repenting of dark sin, getting their lives right with God.

Complacency will go and many people will turn their lives

over to the Lord. As a result, we're going to see outbreaks of joy and the heavy presence of the glory of God.

This is what God wants to release.

I want to ask you, will you yield to him? You fathers, mothers, pastors, missionaries, leaders, worshippers, teachers, entrepreneurs, artists, writers, whoever you are, will you yield and let the Holy Spirit do this through your meetings, your job, and your life? Will you not worry about how you've always done things? Will you bend with the wind of change? Will you walk with the fire of the Holy Spirit? Will you let him come, and will you let him touch his people? Will you breathe with the breath of God, and let him breathe on you?

Let him prophesy and speak through you the words of life. I want to release over you, right now, this renewal of the prophetic voice.

Let me pray for you.

Father, I pray according to your will, that the renewal of the prophetic voice be released to the body of Christ right now. For every leader, for every believer, Lord God, across the world, allow the prophetic voice to rise up inside of them again. May the bubbling of the Holy Spirit rise in them. Empower them not to worry about what it looks like, what it sounds like, or what it feels like. Empower them to release that sound of Heaven that you are releasing, that you will pour out, Father, like a mighty rushing wind on their meetings, on their services, on their families, on their congregations, Lord. Pour out your glory and your latter rain, according to Zechariah 11:1, in a way that we've never seen. Father, I'm so expectant! I'm so excited! I thank you Father, and we come into agreement with you.

Now say this.

Father, I receive the renewal of the prophetic voice and the prophetic dreamer language in my life. In Jesus name. Amen.

There is a restoration of all things at hand. Every time there has been a move of God, it restored the proper functioning of the Body of Christ. Things that had been lost or misinterpreted are rediscovered. Gifts and functions are restored to their original intended glory. God has restored the flow of the gifts of the Spirit through the first wave, a love for the Word of God through the second wave, and the release of true worship through the third wave. Now, in this fourth wave, we will see a restoration of the completed work of God, through all these waves coming together as one and moving as the early church with the Holy Spirit, preaching the full gospel of Jesus Christ and the message of repentance.

THE RESTITUTION OF EVERYTHING

Before Jesus comes back, there has to be a restoration. According to Scripture, in Acts 3:20, 21 (NKJV), we read, *"And that He may send Jesus Christ, who was preached to you before, whom heaven must receive until the times of restoration of all things, which God has spoken by the mouth of all His holy prophets since the world began."*

Wow! The heavens are retaining him, and he is not going to be released until everything is restored back. Don't you think the prophetic dreamers need to be restored back and acknowledged in the Church? Dreams need to be acknowledged in the body of

Christ. Dreams need to be acknowledged in the leadership. I'll tell you why.

God has always spoken to kings through dreams. In the Bible, there are twenty-one different instances where God released a dream to kings and leaders. Eleven of those dreams were in Genesis. Six kings received dreams. King Nebuchadnezzar is one you might know. Daniel was a prophetic voice who dreamed. Joseph, Mary's husband, dreamed and the angel came to him and warned him not to leave Jerusalem. There were four different dreams that protected the baby Jesus.

What if they hadn't put heavy weight or vital importance on those dreams? What if they didn't pay attention, or thought these were dreams caused by something they ate? What would have happened? I thank God they listened. God speaks words through dreams and through His dreamers.

Consider Joseph, the son of Jacob, and the dreams that prophesied of his future. He saw the sheaves bowing down to him. God showed him that the tribes of Israel would bow before him one day. The stars and the sun worshipped him, because he would become the rescuer of the nation of Israel.

God could give you one dream. You might think it's little or small, but it could literally shift your whole life to the direction of His perfect will.

We must listen, yield and obey.

I'm asking the Lord for the Spirit of counsel, the Spirit of wisdom, to come on us, to lead us and guide us.

It's the glory of the king to search out a matter. Find out what He might be showing you through dreams. Sometimes there is a delay in the interpretation, because it's not time for you to fully understand it, or it's not time for the dream to manifest that reality yet. Write the vision down, so that you can run at the appointed time.

The Lord is calling forth his prophets in this season. He's calling us by name. He's calling us by region. He's calling us by country. He is calling our names. The Lord showed me the renewal in the prophetic voice that He is releasing right now. This series of dreams that I have shared with you from May 2018 has given us a glimpse of what we are seeing and what we are going to see.

5

THE PROPHETS ARE CALLED

GOD IS CALLING people to step into being a prophet over their region, or their city, or their own neighborhood. God is calling people into this office, to come into agreement with the Word of the Lord. The prophets of old, like Jeremiah and Isaiah, heard the voice of God clearly. They would always say, *"The word of the Lord came unto me saying...,"* then they would decree the word of the Lord over the land. Not one Word of the Lord would fall to the ground. God is calling people to this office, to know who they are and to be confident in the Lord. But they are not always confident when God first calls.

When God called Jeremiah, He said, *"Before I formed you in the womb I knew you; Before you were born I sanctified you; I ordained you a prophet to the nations."* Jeremiah replied to the Lord, *"Ah, Lord God! Behold, I cannot speak, for I am a youth"* (Jeremiah 1: 5,6 NKJV). Jeremiah didn't believe he had the ability to be what he was called to be. How many of you have felt that way? I know I have. Plenty of times.

Look how God answers Jeremiah, *"Do not say, 'I am a youth,' For you shall go to all to whom I send you, And whatever I command you, you shall speak. Do not be afraid of their faces, For I am with you to deliver you, says the Lord"* (Jeremiah 1:7,8 NKJV).

First, God deals with Jeremiah's fears and insecurity about his own strength. Then, He reminds him that He will be watching over him. God's strength is sufficient for Jeremiah when he feels like he is inadequate. He is young, but God is with him.

You must confront the fears that have stopped you from listening to the voice of God. He has been calling you since before you were born! Those fears are your enemy, and you must allow the strength of God in you to silence every other voice that comes against the true calling of God and His Word over your life.

I hear the Lord echoing this, "Do not say, 'I am but a youth.' Do not say, 'I am not able, I'm not qualified, I have no skills or abilities,' for I, the Lord, I am able to hold you up in your weakness. My grace is sufficient for you. I have called you forth to declare a thing and see it established."

The Lord has called us, and we know who we are in the Spirit, because our spirit man is renewed day by day. He wakes up knowing who he is and that there are new mercies every day. Still, life tries to get us to stop believing. Circumstances and situations often succeed in getting us to stop believing who we are in Christ. But you're not going to listen to that. No, you are going to tell yourself everyday who you are in Jesus Christ!

The Spirit of God will remind you. That's one of His missions. He is faithful to quicken you to the Word of God and bring what the Lord has said to you into your remembrance.

Sometimes our response to the Lord is Jeremiah's response, when he said, "O Lord God, behold, I cannot speak. I am a youth."

How many of you have given God excuses like this? No matter how many times God has used you to bring His Kingdom in someone's life, there's still a place in your mind that says, "O Lord, can you really use me this time? I have to speak for you again? Are you sure? Have you really called me? Have you really anointed me? I'm just a youth. I'm just a woman. I'm just a man. I'm too old. I'm just a worker. I'm just an intercessor. I just pray in my prayer closet. I just drive a truck. I just work at a clothing store. I'm just this or I'm just that."

Well, God has an answer for you.

"You shall go to all to whom I send you, and whatever I command you, you shall speak. Do not be afraid of their faces, for I am with you to deliver you," says the Lord.

When God has called you, the anointing will descend on you and seal that calling on you. You can't turn from it. You have been commissioned. *"For the gifts and the calling of God are irrevocable"* (Romans 11:29). That means "not able to be changed, reversed, or recovered; final."

Once God deals with the fear, then He proceeds to commission Jeremiah.

"Then, the Lord put forth his hand, and touched my mouth. And the Lord said to me. 'Behold, I have put my words in your mouth. See, I have this day set you over the nations and over the kingdoms, To root out and to pull down, To destroy and to throw down, To build and to plant'" (Jeremiah 1: 9,10 NKJV).

God is calling forth a prophetic people to declare the word of the Lord. People who will agree with him. People who will stand in the place of intercession, who will be faithful to pull up the weeds of the enemy, to sow the seeds of the Word of God, to watch over the crops of the harvest. Surround them with your spirit of prayer, with your spirit of faith, those who stand in the midst of persecution, who stand in the midst of the whirlwind, who stand in the midst of chaos. These will hear the still small voice of God and prophesy the word of the Lord.

God is calling forth the prophets, and He is saying, "Will you be my prophet in the secret place in the spirit?"

I know there are national prophets who give national words. I understand that. But there are other types of prophets who speak to the body of Christ. I operate in that kind of office. I believe the Lord has given me a prophetic anointing for dreams. He prophesied to me to release these words to people. He said they would be on target and timely for the Body of Christ. I've surrendered to my commission. Have you surrendered? Maybe you don't know what you're called to do yet. God will speak His vision to you, and He will not delay.

There is one way to know what you've been called to specifically, even if you haven't had prophecies from others or dreams. You can step back and look at the fruit of how God has used you over time. Recognize where the anointing flows in your life. Then, give honor to it, yield to it, and submit yourself to it. Humble yourself to what God has called you to, whether you feel like it or not. Great shall be your reward!

Once you have decided to commit to your calling wholeheartedly, God may begin to ask you questions, as you co-labor with Him, for His Kingdom to be established in the earth.

The Lord asked Jeremiah, "Jeremiah, what do you see?" And he said, "I see a branch of an almond tree." Then the Lord said to him, "You have seen well, for I am ready to perform My word" (Jeremiah 1:11,12 NKJV).

I'm calling forth the prophets and children of God to arise and begin to build and plant with God in the spirit realm. God is ready to perform His word. It's time to pray in the Holy Spirit, to build, and to plant with the Lord for this next era we are entering into. We must come before the Lord, seek His face, and humble ourselves, and turn from our wicked ways. God promises that He will come and heal our land.

Unity and agreement with God's plan is part of the fourth wave of the dark horses I saw. I received the dream on New Year's Day. It was also during the Hebrew year 5779, which means, "grace and unity to birth the harvest with a double portion anointing." God did exactly that. He called the body of Christ to come together in prayer to birth the harvest. Not reap the harvest, but birth it in the Spirit. We have literally carried the seeds to begin to birth forth the youth harvest.

That's why there's been such a fight about birthing life. There are babies who have a right to life and need to be birthed because they are called and anointed by God to go into the world and harvest it for Jesus Christ. They will carry an amazing revelation of the resurrection power of Jesus Christ, with a gift of faith for miracles.

This is why it's so important for you to shake off fear, recognize the calling on your life, and answer it. There are souls hanging in the valley of decision, and you may be their only hope. We, the Body of Christ, need you.

The fire of God is coming on you fresh again and watering

you by the Living Waters of the Holy Spirit. He is re-firing and quickening you to the Word of God that he's put in you. Some dreams that have been dead in you, that have not been activated, God is now reactivating. Now is the time for the harvest to come forth, and everything you have been designed for, born for, sanctified for, and formed for is coming forth in this season.

We're all coming into maturity. This is the season for the sons and daughters of God to come into maturity with the Holy Spirit. We're laying aside our agendas. It's about the Kingdom! We're coming together, and we're going to see the fruit of the Kingdom of God manifested in this generation.

The Lord is saying to you right now, "Don't be afraid of their faces, for I am with you to deliver you," says the Lord.

Some of you have stepped back because of fear—fear that you didn't know how to walk it out, because of fear of people who would not receive your message, or would not receive you, or would not honor who you are.

But the Lord says, "Do not be afraid, for I will give you the words to speak before them. Do not fear their faces, I am with you wherever you go."

The Lord is giving you permission to release words in the Spirit. He's giving you permission in the secret place. He's giving you hidden treasures to prophesy and decree things in the dark places. He is showing you the hidden treasures, and what the darkness is trying to hide.

God is doing this! He's bringing revelation to the truth. He is opening the eyes of people, and people all around the world are beginning to see this harvest time. It's going to be prophesied everywhere. I see sanctification, holiness, and a fresh baptism of fire coming on this generation.

May God touch your mouth the way He did Jeremiah and Isaiah with a coal of fire, cleansing your lips and releasing the spirit of boldness upon you, for such a time as this, to declare the Word of God and speak the truth in the streets.

Father, I pray, for a spirit of boldness to come upon us, that we would declare your Word as you're giving it to us. Lord, you are full of faith and fire, of love and passion. You're a consuming fire! Baptize us afresh, and put that in us, God, that we would be consumed like you are consumed, that we'd be full of passion and love, full of mercy and grace, the way you are full of those things! Empower us to give people Jesus, Lord, the way you want to give people Jesus.

Lord, I thank you that we are Your sons and daughters, that You have given the authority of Jesus Christ to us. I thank you, Lord, that when we decree Your Word, it will happen, just like Jesus withered the fig tree. He looked at his disciples and said, "I tell you, if you say to this mountain, "Be removed and be cast into the sea,' it can be done for you, if you have faith as a mustard seed, it will be done for you."

Lord, I pray right now that we would step into this mountain-moving faith. In this time, we join together in the Spirit and decree, Lord, "Mountain, move! The mountain of blindness, move! The mountain of deafness, move! The mountain of cold-heartedness, move!

Awaken the heart, Lord, awaken the Church, and awaken the harvest. God is awakening the harvest. We're going to speak to the field, and we're going to speak to the harvest, and we're going to command it to awaken. We're going to welcome the Living Water of God to come in. We're going to speak life. We're going to speak the way Jesus speaks. We're going to speak life to the fields, life in the Spirit, life to the harvest, life to the seeds, and we're going to see it spring up, in Jesus name.

It's time to build! It's time to build, and it's time to plant.

Jesus said, "Do you not say, 'There are still four months and then comes the harvest?' Behold, I say to you, lift up your eyes and look at the fields, for they are already white for harvest!"

Jesus is staring at those fields, longing for the lost. Let us rise up and go get them for Him. Give Him the reward of His suffering. Answer the call to the harvest, for Jesus's sake.

6

THE PROPHETS ANSWER

SO FAR, this all sounds great, right? But so many are stuck in the "questioning" phase that they never move past it to the "going" phase, where they are activated and making actual steps towards their God-given goals. Are you stuck there?

How do I answer God's call?
What moment am I ready?
I will never be accomplished enough to take on such big assignments.
It's too overwhelming and too full of the unknown.
I'm scared to the core.
I'd rather stay safe in my little box and do what I know I can count on.
I wouldn't even know how to begin.
I have no help at all.
What if I fail?
What if I'm not good enough?

What if people reject me?
What if nothing goes right?
Too many things are involved.
It's too hard.
I don't know how to do any of this.

These are all valid questions and thoughts. And maybe they're right. But what if they're wrong?

I would like to approach this idea from another angle.

What if we don't answer the call and give God our yes? Then what? Can you walk through your life saying no after no after no to God? Are you prepared to look Jesus in the eyes, knowing He put dreams in your heart and you never even took one step to pursue them? I don't want that feeling that I could have done more, I could have pushed harder, I could have stepped out in faith, I could have chosen to believe.

I know this place because I've been there. In fact, I lived there for years. Why? Because I never believed *God in me* was enough to do everything that He promised. I didn't believe Him. I didn't believe He really called me, even though He told me again and again and again.

Oh, the mercy and patience of God! He let me feel His love for me over and over. I heard His sweet voice, wooing me into the place of deep love, where deep calls to deep.

Somewhere, in that search for Him, I found who I was. I saw myself through His eyes. That's when I believed that I could do anything!

Satan tried to stop me. I would arise from that place of prayer, only to face the cares of this life and circumstances that would choke out the Word poured into my spirit. Fear arose in my heart again, challenging the faith I carried, and would usually win. I was stuck in this battle between a lie and the truth. What will I believe? What will I agree with and choose in the end? Tossed to and fro on the sea of decision, I wrestled. The lie was just strong enough to keep me from jumping out of the boat onto the sea of faith and go to Jesus, once and for all, completely devoted to Him alone—no more wavering, and never turning back.

DID GOD TRULY CALL ME?

If we are insecure and in unbelief about God's calling on our life, then He will continually comfort and uplift us. He continually reminded me of why He created me and the pleasure He has in my love for Him. He whispered all the things I would do in the future, things I could not digest at the moment. He believed in me!

He knows that the strength He puts within us through His son Jesus Christ is more than enough. It's the resurrection power of God that wakes us out of death, out of sleep, and we rise to His voice, just like Lazarus arose from the grave at the sound of His Master and Friend. Lazarus awoke and came out of death and darkness. Jesus calls to you now—"Awake! Come forth!"

If there is death, come out of it. If there is darkness, come out of it. Enter into the Life of Jesus, and His Light.

That Life and Light will turn all those questions into answers, if you will wait on Him, trust Him, lean into Him. He will say, *"I have called you for such a time as this. You have everything you need already inside you. You have my heart and my voice to guide you. I will lead you on the path of life, and you will see My glory. I will never leave you or forsake you. All things work together for good for those who love Me. When you seek Me and My righteousness, everything else will be added to you. Do not be afraid, for I am with you wherever you go."*

"*Faith is the substance of things hoped for and the evidence of things not seen*" (Hebrews 11:1 NKJV). You must not draw back. Make a choice to believe that if God has spoken it, then it shall come to pass. You must become determined not to lose your ground from this stance. Stand strong in His might, and let God be your strength, even in your weaknesses. He is faithful to hold you up even when you feel like you might faint. You must know this, and believe this with all your heart. Do not waver, ever. No matter what. You stand.

I KNOW I'M CALLED

Some people are in a different situation. They have been strong in the belief of what they have been called to do, but as they have pursued it they have had no success. There can be many reasons for this outcome for many sons and daughters of God.

There are seasons of waiting. If this is you, you must trust that He knows your times and seasons best, and He will not fail in the release of His Word over your life. For some of you, it may have been years or even decades since God showed you great and mighty things in your future.

Remember that Joseph was shown through two dreams that he would be worshipped as a king. As a youth, he was so excited to tell his family about the dream God gave him, of the wheat bowing to him. In another dream, the sun and stars bowed to him. He was convinced God was speaking a mystery that would unfold in due time. I'm sure Joseph thought it would be sooner rather than later. And I'm also sure that it was way later than he would have liked! He went through terrible situations, the first when he was sold by his own brothers into slavery. Then things finally looked a little better, and he was promoted to serve a wealthy man, Potiphar. But then the man's wife lied and said Joseph attacked her. He was thrown into prison for twenty years!

Joseph must have been thinking, *What? I thought I was the chosen one. I thought You were raising me up to do great things for You, God. I would be given a kingdom to rule. Why have you forsaken me? I have done nothing wrong. I don't deserve this!*

Can you imagine what Joseph must have been feeling?

Have you felt this way and had a similar conversation with God?

If we think we know who we are, even from a youth, and a little pride is mixed in, we may, like Joseph, become crushed for a season. The Bible says, *For everyone who exalts himself will be humbled, and he who humbles himself will be exalted* (Luke 14:11). *Pride goes before destruction, and a haughty spirit before stumbling* (Proverbs 16:18). Having those dreams, it was natural for Joseph to think much of himself at first. I bet he felt pretty special to God. But after the hardships he suffered, he was humbled. Finally, when a baker and cupbearer arrived in that prison cell needing interpretation of their dreams, Joseph could have been bitter. Instead, he chose to help them. God saw it, and it was good.

At the lowest place in his life, Joseph was a blessing. Little did he know that it would be the very reason he was delivered from that prison and brought straight into Pharaoh's court, where God gave him favor to become second in command over all of Egypt.

Be careful. Pride is a trap setter. But thanks be to God, He pulls us out of those traps with His merciful right hand. And He doesn't give up on us. *For I am confident of this very thing, that He who began a good work in you will perfect it until the day of Christ Jesus* (Philippians 1:6). He is the God of many second chances!

MATURE FRUIT

Maybe you have a heart of gold, and no spot or blemish is in you. In this case, you must trust that God has an appointed time for your fruit to mature, when your gift will taste the sweetest. Fruit picked too early is sour and hard. But with time, it is softened and becomes oh so sweet!

Maybe this is you. Your heart has softened, and your voice has sweetened through the ripening of life. God will pluck you at the perfect time, and the world will taste and see God's goodness through you.

I remember when I thought I was ready to progress in my calling, and that my tree was producing good fruit. I was given dreams and words from well-known leaders. I thought for sure, this was it. God is commissioning me to a higher place! Time passed, and my hope began to wane. I thought that maybe I missed it somewhere, maybe I didn't hear God. I was heartbroken. My spirit was so low.

As years passed by, God continued to comfort me and reassure me that He had a work for me to accomplish. We wrestled often! Jacob wrestled God, you know, until God blessed him. I believe I too can go before the throne of grace and obtain mercy for my life. When the time of my promised season arrived, I had learned the place of contentment. It's in my salvation alone. God walked me through a valley of isolation and pain and sorrow, until I learned to grab onto Him and never let go. He was all I had. In that journey, I fell so much more in love with Him that I finally saw what He was trying to get across to me. He is all I need. When opportunities for me to minister began to present themselves after that, I did not want it! I had found the one whom my soul loved, and I did not want to let go.

God began to talk to my heart. He revealed that, because I no longer sought after anything but Him, He would promote me before others so that they too could hear the beat of His heart. They would awaken to His love and become completely His. Our God is a jealous God, and He will have no other gods before Him.

I pray that you too will find this place of surrender. Shut down every other voice but His, and find true rest. You could gain the whole world, but lose your own soul. My friend, it's not worth it. Let go of your agenda, and let heaven's agenda take over your life. His yoke is easy and His burden is light.

THE TIMING OF YOUR PROMISE

One thing is certain. God is good, and He is faithful to perform His Word that He has spoken. Maybe it's to come forth right now, maybe in a few years. Rest assured, it will surely come. Wait for it. Wait on the Lord.

Isaiah 55:11 (NKJV) says, *So shall My word be that goes forth from My mouth; It shall not return to Me void, But it shall accomplish what I please, And it shall prosper in the thing for which I sent it.* Guess what? You are a word that God spoke forth into the earth. You went forth from His mouth. You will not return void, but accomplish what He pleases and prosper in the things where He sent you. Your destiny is in that word.

We have literally been birthed from the mouth of God. That is amazing! And we have a promise from God, that what He speaks forth over us cannot be voided.

Did you hear that? Your calling cannot be stopped. Go ahead and step right into it, because you will not fail. If you have built your house on the rock of Christ, then no matter what comes against you, you will stand.

I've had to walk this truth out in my own life. When I saw nothing in the natural realm of what I saw in the spiritual realm, I had to continue to believe that God is truth, and He cannot lie to me. He would not say something that He would not do. I went back and forth with doubt and faith quite often. Still, I hung onto the prophetic promises, even when it seemed like my boat was sinking.

God knew there was a season I was being prepared for, and I had to believe that He knew best. And I still do. I haven't seen everything I've been told, but it will surely come to pass, just as I've watched His faithful hand over and over fulfill prayers and dreams of my heart.

The Bible says, *You will show me the path of life; In Your presence is fullness of joy; At Your right hand are pleasures forevermore* (Psalm 16:11 NKJV).

This is the secret. The pleasure of knowing Him. Not running a business, or ministry, or whatever you do in life. In His presence is fullness! Seek after this with all your heart, and then every other thing you do will flow from this completed state of the pleasure of knowing Him.

DON'T RUN

Maybe you are someone who has been running and hasn't answered the call of the Lord. It's no coincidence that you picked up this book. If you want to run the race that God has destined for you to run, I want you to know that I am here cheering you on. People are being touched everywhere through my ministry, and I thank God that I said yes. For Jesus sake! He is establishing His kingdom in hearts all over the world, and I'm honored to be part of pouring out His heart to you. I know that there's no distance in the Spirit. As I have been praying and releasing this word, it's releasing the truth in you and throughout the body of Christ.

You are part of God's gigantic plan, for the Kingdom to be preached to every living creature. You must heed this call. I pray for the leaders in every part of society that they would awaken to the gospel, awaken to Jesus, and become the revolutionists God is looking for in this time. Let us release the prayers of incense that will overflow the bowls of Revelation 5:8. Let's fast and pray for the leaders of the nations. God is preparing and activating the harvesters of souls. I believe that the seeds we have planted have been part of the awakening blooming right now in the earth.

There was a season when God was dealing with me to answer His call in a deeper way in my own life, after He had already opened doors for ministry opportunities. I thought I had answered the call already. I was travelling and speaking, seeing miracles, healings, deliverance and salvation everywhere I went. I was receiving dreams for people as words of knowledge. I was praying, fasting, and weeping in worship every day. I was sold out and deeply in love. Surely I was in complete obedience! But there was more that God wanted me to press into.

He wanted me to awaken the heart of a people, of a church, of a nation. God would not choose me for such a task, I thought. Like He wouldn't choose a fifteen-year old shepherd boy to one day be King of Israel. But He did!

Can we believe God, that He calls us to do things beyond our comprehension, beyond our capabilities, beyond our skills, and beyond our human reach? What if we choose to believe for the greater things God shows us? Did I want a bigger ministry, a bigger reach, to be seen of men? God forbid. I feared the place of self-exaltation. In fact, I ran from it. But God, who is so rich in mercy, saw my heart and wanted me to reach further. He called me. He gave me the dreams. His voice superseded every preconceived notion I had imagined. He called me out of those fears, because He saw the heart of a little girl, who from the age of six-years old has loved Him and His Word. He saw a girl who was tender hearted and loved people deeply. He saw the faithfulness in my heart, and He knew He could trust me.

God sees your heart, too. He sees you in the field alone, worshipping and adoring Him. He knows you love the audience of One more than anyone else. And for this reason, He will call you out and put you before others, to display what a true worshipper looks like to Him.

It looks a lot like you.

WHEN I ANSWERED THE CALL TO "AWAKEN THE HEART"

I heard a call that I never asked for. The Lord gave me three dreams, and they were a prophetic word for me to awaken the heart. I didn't understand them at first. God often speaks in riddles.

The Lord spoke to me in the first dream and said, "It's time to awaken the heart."

I woke, not understanding what that meant for me to do. God doesn't give us dreams so we can get goosebumps and say, "Wow." He has a purpose behind what He speaks.

So I asked, "What does this mean, Lord? What do you want me to do?"

Within a week, I had another dream. God said, "It's time to awaken the church."

I saw schools of the Spirit being overtaken with the outpouring of the Holy Spirit, and they could not go on as usual. A fire was lit within them. I saw chaos happening all over the place, as people worshipped wildly, prophesied, prayed, wept on the floor, and danced all around. It looked like revival. I woke and said, "Lord, what does this mean? And why are you showing this to me? I need more instruction. What do you want me to do?"

Have you ask Him this question? *God, what do you want me to do?*

I stayed in prayer, waiting on the Lord until I received the final dream, which came with instructions. What a relief! I was given some details.

Do you need details for God's plan for your life?

In this dream, I heard God say, "If you want to see local revival, you have to start with soaking sessions."

I woke up from this thinking, *What? Revival from soaking sessions? How?*

Because I fear God and completely trusted that He would answer my questions, I chose to obey. I began to wonder what this would look like, and how I would do it. Listen friends, God oftentimes doesn't give us the complete blueprint. He reveals only the next step in our journey. He enjoys teaching us faith and trust. He loves leading us and is so pleased when we follow. Have faith that God knows what He's doing, and you don't need to know every single detail. Follow Him.

I inquired of the Lord what he wanted to happen in these sessions. I said, *Lord, I don't have a building, but I do have a plat-form on social media where I could do live video prayer and soaking sessions.*

That night, December 16, 2017, I walked outside to watch the Geminids meteor shower as I pondered this decision. I watched tiny lights streak across the sky, and I continued in prayer.

Then, I became very bold and said, *God, you don't have to do this, but would you mind confirming that I should start these soaking sessions on social media by letting me see the biggest meteor I've ever seen?*

I thought surely it won't happen, and then I won't have to do videos. I really didn't want to do them. I was too insecure to believe that God could use me in media ministry. Yet my spirit wrestled within me, because it knows who I really am.

After asking God this outrageous question, I assumed that an answer would be immediate. Nothing happened. I was released, right? Free from doing something I was unsure of.

I turned to walk down the hill. I walked up to Munday and put my arm within his. We both looked up at the sky, and in that very moment we saw the brightest streak of fire drop straight down, as if it fell from heaven itself. It continued until it split into three individual pieces, which continued to streak the sky until finally fading. My jaw dropped and my spirit leaped. I realized I had just been commissioned by heaven! It was confirmed by this sign. Does God use signs? Absolutely. And "Awaken the Heart" saturation sessions were born.

Not long after I started on January 11, 2018, I began to see a trend. People were using the term *awakening* or *awaken* as a common thread. Within months it became the main theme for many Christian events. God gave me "Awaken the Heart" before it was popular, before the word *awaken* showed up in the main conference title of so many different ministries.

I love that! God used me as a catalyst, as a forerunner of this awakening in the Spirit. I believe something was released when I said yes, and it caused a tidal wave of movement. I asked the Lord to send me people who would join with me in the Spirit, in agreement with God's promises to manifest in the earth. I said, *God, give me a small group of people who are hungry and on fire. People of faith who will pray and decree Your Word.*

He answered my prayer. God sent me many spear-throwing warriors. We may look like a small army, but a small army can do so much. Remember Gideon's army of 300, when God called them to overtake their enemy, the Midianites. It was impossible to defeat their enemy because of the great number. The Midianites must've had quite an army! We read that 22,000 of Israel's army fled and returned home due to fear of dying. Only 10,000 remained to fight.

God told Gideon, *"The people who are with you are too many for Me to give Midian into their hands, for Israel would become boastful, saying, 'My own power has delivered me.'"* And Gideon *"brought the people down to the water. And the Lord said to Gideon, "You shall separate everyone who laps the water with his tongue as a dog laps, as well as everyone who kneels to drink." Now the number of those who lapped, putting their hand to their mouth, was 300 men; but all the rest of the people kneeled to drink water. The Lord said to Gideon, "I will deliver you with the 300 men who lapped and will give the Midianites into your hands;"*

"Now the same night it came about that the Lord said to him, "Arise, go down against the camp, for I have given it into your hands. But if you are afraid to go down, go with Purah your servant down to the camp, and you will hear what they say; and afterward your hands will be strengthened that you may go down against the camp. When Gideon came, behold, a man was relating a dream to his friend. And he said, "Behold, I had a dream; a loaf of barley bread was tumbling into the camp of Midian, and it came to the tent and struck it so that it fell, and turned it upside down so that the tent lay flat." His friend replied, "This is nothing less than the sword of Gideon the son of Joash, a man of Israel; God has given Midian and all the camp into his hand."

"When Gideon heard the account of the dream and its interpretation, he bowed in worship. He returned to the camp of Israel and said, "Arise, for the Lord has given the camp of Midian into your hands" (Judges 7:2, 5-7, 9-11, 13-15).

A dream brought the message of the Lord to His people. Listening to the dream brought victory over the enemy. God gave me a dream, and I listened. Now He has formed this army to overthrow the enemy in our land for His glory. We pray and see victory, because we follow His voice and His Word. Then we speak that Word forth by prophesying it.

When you prophesy, when the Holy Spirit comes on you and you're releasing things in the Spirit, you know that things are happening. Don't just hope God hears you and that your prayers might be answered. You don't need to run in fear from the trials you face before you. God hears you, and He will answer. You will not fail. You will have the victory in the fight that lays before you, just like Gideon's army. God is with you. Who can be against you?

I pray you hear the Father's voice rising up in your spirit today. It's time for you to hear God, however He wants to speak to you—through dreams, visions, prophetic words, and above all through His Word. Let's listen and answer God, the way He listens and answers us. Are you ready to answer this call? Receive the baton and run the race laid before you, the course laid out before you were even born.

I want to challenge you to make this choice today. Choose to follow hard after God and His plan for you. Make the steps daily you need to reach that goal. Will you take this challenge? If you say yes, then you must not look back. Let's do this. Remember, the Bible says, *"For I know the plans I have for you," declares the Lord, "plans to prosper you and not to harm you, plans to give you hope and a future"* (Jeremiah 29:11 NIV).

DId you hear that? He has the plans already in His hands. Run with it!

You are going to see things shift and shake. You will be a catalyst for the next season in the body of Christ. Maybe you won't know it. Maybe your name won't be stamped on it. But that's okay, because when you get to heaven the Lord is going to say, *These are the seeds you've planted. Look at the fruit of your labor. Look at what your faith grew. Look at the harvest that came forth from your mustard seed faith.*

You are going to fulfill the will of God. You will hear His voice. You will answer His call. You will say yes. This is the season, when God calls and the prophets answer. Now, when God calls, *you* answer.

7

REBIRTH YOUR DREAMS

I HEAR some of you thinking, *How do I answer a call when I have nothing? My dreams are gone. They died long ago because my hope was deferred and I grew weary and I fainted. My dreams are dead.*

But I say to you, your dreams are not dead, only asleep. They've laid dormant in the hands of the enemy, who came to sift you out from the harvest fields. He came to steal your passion, your fire, and your destiny. He thinks if he can wear you down enough, that you will quit. Are you going to let him win? Are you going to lay down defeated, waving a white flag?

Or, are you ready to stand up? And after all that you've done, you keep standing.

God has a promise for you, and His promises are yes and amen. I'm writing this to stir you up and shake you until you can't sit still any longer. God is faithful. He wants you to believe and watch His glory move. It's time to rebirth your dreams!

Sometimes we believe something is dead when it is only asleep. Matthew tells us, *the synagogue official came and bowed down before Him, and said, "My daughter has just died; but come and lay Your hand on her, and she will live." When Jesus came into the official's house, and saw the flute-players and the crowd in noisy disorder, He said, "Leave; for the girl has not died, but is asleep." And they began laughing at Him* (Matthew 9:18, 23, 24).

Your dreams are not dead, as you suppose, they are only asleep. Let Jesus take you by the hand, and rise. The resurrection power of Jesus Christ will awaken these dreams right now!

Blessed are those who hunger and thirst for righteousness, for they shall be satisfied. (Matthew 5:6) The Word of God is true for us today. We are going to see so much blessing and favor upon our lives because we're after the Lord's heart.

A REVISITED SOUND

I want to share a dream I had July 7, 2018. I saw John and Carol Arnott, the leaders of the Father's Blessing in Toronto, Canada, that we discussed earlier in the book. I've never dreamed about them before. The Lord has been impressing upon my heart that He's going to revisit what He did there, and we will see another high praise movement, with much joy, deliverance, restoration, and healings.

Why did I have this dream on 7/7? We will get to that in a minute. I was watching John and Carol and they were so full of the joy of the Lord. They knew that something had broken through. Something had come forth in the Spirit that they had longed to see in the body of Christ again. All of a sudden I heard in the background a song begin to play, and before me a scroll was laid out, with lyrics on it. I looked and I knew in my spirit that this was a song that had been written during that outpouring of the Father's blessing. I didn't recognize the song. I was aware that I was looking at a very anointed song. The Lord said to me, there's going to be a rebirth of a song or songs that were released during that time. We're going to hear these songs come forth and they're going to be fresh. It's a new sound with a fresh wind upon the songs and/or sound that was released during that time. I don't know if it's one song, or a series of songs, or the sound of worship itself. Maybe it's the sound or the Spirit of the music.

THE SOUND IN YOU

God is rebirthing a sound in the earth and He is rebirthing a sound in you. He is waking you and causing you to hope and dream of all His promises today. He reminds you that all of His promises are not forgotten. All of his promises are yes and amen. All of his promises are sure. *Jesus Christ is the same yesterday and today and forever.* (Hebrews 13:8) Whatever he's spoken to you, it will come to pass. The Word that God has spoken over your life will happen. The Lord wants you to dream with him. Remember how I said, *we can get stuck in the questioning?* Choose today to move past the questions, even without all the answers.

Move out and follow your fire. What do you burn for? Most of the time, this is what you were designed to fulfill. God wants to release the river of living water and open up to you again, but the questioning has caused you to get stuck. God wants to confirm and assure us today.

Choose to believe—*Yes, I am called. Yes, this is what I'm passionate about. Yes, this is what I'm supposed to move in. Yes, the anointing will move through my life.*

No more tossing to and fro friends. Jump out of the boat of questions once and for all, then turn around and burn that boat! Swim into the deep. Be confident of what He has called you to do. Stop allowing insecurity, rejection and inferior feelings to stop you from moving forward.

People are drowning out at sea, while you safely float in the boat of complacency and disobedience. Whoa, did I just write that? Yes, that is what all of these things boil down to—*laziness and disobedience.* I lived in these boats for years, and I had to burn them down. You can too. It only takes one spark of fire, lit by the flame of your love. Make that decision today.

It's time to let the rebirth come alive inside of you. It's time to dig up that old dream you thought was dead. You thought God wasn't going to use you or move through you, so you gave up. You weren't seeing anything happen, and you got frustrated and disappointed. *Hope deferred makes the heart sick..* (Proverbs 13:12)

YOUR DREAM IS NOT DEAD

A girl died, and all the people were weeping around her. Jesus showed up and said, "Stop weeping, for she has not died, but is asleep" (Luke 8:52). So I say to those of you who are weeping now, your dream is not dead, it's only asleep. And Jesus has sent me to wake you up, to wake your dream up!

I'm here to encourage you with the fire of God. And He is pouring out His fire on this! I know you feel it.

God is saying: *Arise, awaken your calling. I am in you. It's time to let that dream be reborn. It's time to let it experience rebirth. It's time to let it breathe inside of you again. It's time to hope again. It's time to get up and get unstuck from the questioning.*

Stick to the going! Move in your calling and giftings. Don't look for another teaching, or another seminar, or another class. All those things are great, all those things are wonderful. I know that they help us grow, but be "in the going," even while you're listening to teachings. Don't listen to teachings then question what you're called to do. The Lord has put inside of you what you are called to do. I guarantee that your spirit will bear witness with the Holy Spirit what you are created to move in. You should burn for it!

I know what I burn for—I burn to pray. I burn to worship.

And we are all called to be true worshipers, according to John 4:23. *But an hour is coming, and now is, when the true worshipers will worship the Father in spirit and truth; for such people the Father seeks to be His worshipers.* You are called to worship the Father. You're called to worship Jesus. That's your number one calling. We should desire this communion with Him above all.

No matter what God is calling you to in our culture, there is one goal for it all: to reconcile people to God. Whatever you do, reconcile people to Him, however you can. Enjoy the process of knowing Him and making Him known.

ARE GIFTS LIMITED?

Don't limit God in the way He will move through you. The Bible says, *Now there are varieties of gifts, but the same Spirit. And there are varieties of ministries, and the same Lord. There are varieties of effects, but the same God who works all things in all persons. But to each one is given the manifestation of the Spirit for the common good. For to one is given the word of wisdom through the Spirit, and to another the word of knowledge according to the same Spirit; to another faith by the same Spirit, and to another gifts of healing by the one Spirit, and to another the effecting of miracles, and to another prophecy, and to another the distinguishing of spirits, to another various kinds of tongues, and to another the interpretation of tongues. But one and the same Spirit works all these things, distributing to each one individually just as He wills* (1 Corinthians 12:4-11).

Did you hear that? The Spirit distributes to each one as He wills. He will cause you to move in whatever gifting He desires. Believe that there are no limitations. The Bible doesn't say you can only move in one gift. Nor does it say you can only have two gifts. In fact, I see nowhere at all where it gives guidelines as to how many gifts an individual can move in. Don't limit God! He can speak to you in many ways and work through you for others in a variety of gifts.

He will empower you to move in every gift, as He wills. That is the key point, "as He wills." He will let you move in words of wisdom, words of knowledge, and gifts of healing. He will let you work miracles and prophecy. He will give you tongues and interpretation of tongues. God is rebirthing dreams inside of us, because there is a renewal in the prophetic voice. He wants you to use your gifts.

> *Test Me now in this," says the LORD of hosts, "if I will not open for you the windows of heaven and pour out for you a blessing until it overflows* (Malachi 3:10).

Let God bless you! Let Him overflow through you. You are his beloved. You are His child. He has put great things in you. You carry treasures inside. You have diamonds in you. You need to believe in that. You can move with the Lord. Too often we stop moving with the Holy Spirit, because we question whether we hear or sense Him.

I want to give you some good advice. Become like a little child. Jesus said, *"Truly I say to you, unless you are converted and become like children, you will not enter the kingdom of heaven"* (Matthew 18:3). Children trust. Children believe all things. They don't doubt that their mom and dad will provide for them. They don't question that they will be there for them in whatever they need. Like a little child, we need to believe in Him. Have faith that He will move and speak through you.

Jesus wanted His disciples to have a gift, so He breathed on them and said, *"Receive the Holy Spirit"* (John 20:22). Jesus wants us to receive the gift of the Holy Spirit. He said, *"So if you who are evil know how to give good gifts to your children, how much more will your Father in heaven give the Holy Spirit to those who ask Him!"* (Luke 11:13 NKJV). It says, *"But if any of you lacks wisdom, let him ask of God, who gives to all generously and without reproach, and it will be given to him."* (James 1:5) It sounds simple to move with the Holy Spirit. You have permission. You've been given everything you need.

It's time to see the body rising up in the faith of a child, in celebration of the Father's love. It's time to go out into the city. People don't know that God will show up to them today, through you. It's time to let God rebirth in you the things that you burn for. It's time to let it out. It's time to move. You're going to see great things happen. You're going to see salvations, people giving their heart to Jesus, getting delivered, emotional and physical healings, miracles on the streets, and so much more.

The Holy Spirit is on you. He is with you. He is ready to move through you. Oh, that someone would yield to the Holy

Spirit! Oh, that we would move with Him! I wonder how much we would see, if we would move with the Holy Spirit. What would happen, if everywhere we go we look and watch with the Lord.

I am a watchman. You are a watchman. The Lord will give you your own watch, and He wants you to watch the people around you and see how He will move upon them. The Lord desires for you to believe in yourself and not hold back.

Listen, I was the shy insecure little girl who never said a word. I wouldn't step out in faith. Oh, that I would have believed in myself for all those years. How much could I have done for Jesus? I thought, *I'm the quiet one. I'm the shy one. I don't have eloquence of speech. I have nothing to give to others. I don't have the gift of the word of knowledge.* The list of reasons was endless.

I used to watch my husband, Munday, give words of knowledge, and I'd think, *Wow, that's amazing. I wish I could do that.* For years I limited what God could do in me. Munday had to shake me out of that place of thinking that I couldn't do it. He encouraged me to step out in faith and believe. I'm so thankful he didn't give up on me. God didn't either.

We reap what we sow, and God gives the increase. Sow what little you think you have, and God will bring the increase as you remain faithful to give to others. If you keep going, keep asking, keep sowing, God will multiply your seed sown and increase the fruits of your righteousness (2 Corinthians 9:10).

It's such a deception to believe that certain people are anointed to prophesy and others aren't. Paul said, *Pursue love, yet desire earnestly spiritual gifts, but especially that you may prophesy* (1 Corinthians 14:1). All can prophesy, but we must follow after love.

Prophecy is a gift for all to express. I didn't move in it because I thought it was for a certain few. The Bible tells us, *But one and the same Spirit works all these things, distributing to each one individually just as He wills* (1 Corinthians 12:11). What if he wills to give to you each gift at different times? We can all move in the nine gifts of the Spirit, but we move in different ones at different times, because it's the Lord's gift and it's His anointing. It's not something you turn on and off.

There are times when the Lord won't let me prophesy. He gives me nothing, because sometimes He's doing something else. Sometimes he's doing a baptism of the Holy Spirit. Sometimes he's doing a deep work in someone, and he doesn't want me to give a word of knowledge and distract the deepness going on in their spirit. The Lord has stopped me many times and said, *No, do not prophesy. Do not touch them. Do not talk to them, because I'm doing something in them.* A holy fear will come on me at that moment.

There are other times where the Holy Spirit will pour out the spirit of prophecy in the room. I'm able to prophesy to each person detailed words of knowledge, physical ailments that they're going through, emotional trauma that they've been through, and many things about their lives. The Lord pours it out, because He wants to heal them.

Is it me? Is it a gift I carry? No. It's listening to the will of the Father. *Lord, do you have a word for them?* I listen. I'm in communication. I'm thinking. I'm listening. I'm hearing. I'm feeling. Then, I begin to move as He moves. I don't force prophecy. Sometimes the Lord doesn't allow me to pray for somebody, because He is touching them. Oftentimes I don't lay hands on people, because it's what the Lord is doing.

We have to be led by the Holy Spirit. Breaking the tradition of what our minds are conditioned to follow is very important to move with the Holy Spirit. What if the Lord doesn't want to do what we are planning? Maybe He wants to do a corporate baptism of fire. What if He wants to do a corporate baptism of love? What if He wants to release the angelic realm and give people encounters with Jesus? We have to be led by the Holy Spirit.

Let God rebirth in you the desire and dream to move with the Holy Spirit. Have faith like a child and yield to the Holy Spirit. I feel God's heart about this so strong. It's time to rebirth and come forth. You are powerful, you are anointed, and you are chosen by God.

Pray this prayer with me right now.

Father, I ask you to release me from disappointment and circumstances that have tried to shut me down. Break the chains of the enemy that bring a veil of darkness and unbelief over me. Set me free from the lies of insecurity and rejection, especially rejecting myself. Release your love, Lord. Let me know how much you believe in me. Let me feel your heart. Show me that what you've put in me is not dead and gone. It's alive and well. Thank you for pouring the water and fire of your Holy Spirit into the depths of my being. You have given me everything I need to go. Let the faith that moves mountains be released inside of me today. I grab my dreams and won't let go, because these are mine, given to me by you, my loving Heavenly Father, I stretch forth my hand and run with Your dreams. In Jesus name. Amen.

I hear the Lord say, *As you go, preach, saying the Kingdom of heaven is at hand. And I will increase your anointing as you give. I will release the fire of My Spirit upon you, and it will increase. The more you give, the more that pours out to you. You may not feel fire right now, but if you will stretch forth your hand to the broken, to the needy, I will come and rescue your soul, heal your brokenness, and restore to you all the years that were lost. I will redeem the time for you. Stretch forth your hand. Run with this command, and you will see Me arise over you with healing in My wings. I will increase the fruits of your righteousness and multiply your seed sown. Watch and see what I will do. Be willing and obedient, and you will eat the fruit of the land. You have permission and you are commissioned this day. Go!*

8

RESTITUTION IS AT HAND

THERE IS a new release in the prophetic realm for you to operate in right now. Go out, step into it, and see the Lord open up heaven and pour out such a blessing that it overflows all over you.

Do you believe it? Do you believe he's put things inside of you that you haven't seen come to fruition? Do you believe that God can release a prophetic shift over your life? Could there be real change and real fruit taking place right now? I dare you to believe it. Take God at His Word.

We are experiencing a shaking. Everything has come to a climax in the Spirit—there is a breaking forth right now. I saw this a few years ago in a dream, when the Spirit of God spoke through me as I prophesied to the church. I said, "Everything is coming to a head! The restitution of all things is at hand!"

God reminded me of this Scripture, "*...and that He may send Jesus, the Christ appointed for you, whom heaven must receive*

UNTIL the period of restoration of all things about which God spoke by the mouth of His holy prophets from ancient time" (Acts 3:20, 21). Jesus will not return UNTIL the restoration of all things. There is one mission, one hope of our calling, one purpose, and that is to reconcile the world to God through Christ. The Father is waiting for the fulness of Christ to be formed in His Body so that this appointed time may come.

God has always called His people through the mouths of prophets, and He continues to do the same today. If we will not hear them, or if the prophets refuse to speak His Word, then He will raise up others who aren't afraid to preach the full gospel of Jesus Christ— repentance of sin and the reconciliation of the world through the Blood of Jesus.

The restitution of all things is at hand. God is restoring the message of the cross and turning from sin, and He is calling you to be one of His voices to speak His Words of Life to a lost generation on their way to hell. Will you heed His call? Will you let your dreams to serve God with all your heart be reborn in you and rebirth the passion to follow Jesus in complete obedience? I believe you will.

THE ANOINTING IS INCREASING FOR THE HARVEST

I dreamed recently that the Presence of Jesus will be felt by believers and unbelievers alike, because Jesus is coming closer to us every day. He wants to reveal Himself to all of us. He wants the lost to feel His heart for them, so that they will run to Him. He is revealing His glory to all flesh in all the earth. Many will resist Him, but many will receive Him.

In the dream, Jesus took another step toward earth every day.

As the day of His return approaches, His glory will get stronger and stronger. That's what He revealed to me. People will feel an anointing as we weep together in His great love. I don't know about you, but when I feel Jesus, I can't control the weeping, it pours out of my heart. I want Him more than anything in this world. I really do. And I tell Him all the time, I hope you know how much I love you, Jesus. I know He feels the same way about us. Oh, if we knew the depths of His love, we would always run straight into His arms!

This increase of His Presence is so that the whole world will see and know that Jesus is Lord. It's for the lost, so that they may know Him and have eternal life. His Presence convicts us of our sins, so that we will come out of the darkness, which separates us from His great love, and enter into His glorious Light.

This is why we must allow the Holy Spirit to move through us in signs, wonders, and miracles. We must reach this broken world. That is what God wants. He wants every heart to be His forever.

You will release a word of knowledge over people that will cause them to make a decision. They will say, I know God must be real, because there's no way they could know that about me. It will force them to make a decision—either they're going to serve God or they're not, because the knowledge of the glory of the Lord is covering the earth. He will reveal that to them. Now is the time. We're here. This is it. The glory is exploding in places. We are in it!

I hear the Holy Spirit asking this of every church body I go to. I hear him asking, *What do you want? Do you want this outpouring? Do you want this Awakening? Do you want this in your life? Do you want to really see me move with the winds of change and shift the atmosphere in your city? Do you really want it, because if you do, he's saying he will give it to you, but you have to give him your everything.*

You have to say yes, Lord. You must yield to the Holy Spirit and make room for him. Jesus is coming, I am telling you. I feel it. We are in the season of it. Sure, I know it could be decades. It could be a century. I don't know when he's going to come back, but what I do know is that NOW is the time to prepare the way of the Lord.

GET READY TO BE INTERRUPTED

I feel like the voice of one crying in the wilderness, like John the Baptist. Get ready, make room in your home. If you know a guest is coming over, you get ready. You put the oil in your lamp. You clean the house. You prepare. So get the food ready, because your guest, the Lord, the master of the house, is coming. If we really believe the Lord is coming to our congregations, to our cities, to the church, then we need to get ready. We can't keep sitting back, thinking we have time.

We must go into the streets and call people to get ready. It's time to prepare the temple of the Lord. Prepare yourself. The Lord is coming to visit you. The Lord is coming to visit people who don't know he's coming to visit them.

There is no stopping this wind of change. God is about to visit every ministry and church. But they still get to choose whether they will move with the winds of change or stay with their customs and traditions. God wants to move in your life, in worship, during the message time, and during the altar call time.

When people pray for you, don't limit how God can minister

to you. The Lord is wanting to move powerfully in His people. He wants you to have encounters. Some will experience heavenly visions and trances. The Lord is going to take people up to heaven. Little children are going to have encounters, even while the service is ending. They will see Jesus and the Father. Are we ready for this? Can we expect things like this?

Too often we don't expect that the Lord can or will do these things. But it's time to shake everything off and start watching and seeing what the Lord will do. *"I will stand on my guard post And station myself on the rampart; And I will keep watch to see what He will speak to me, And how I may reply when I am reproved"* (Habakkuk 2:1). It's time to station ourselves and watch what the Lord does during the service. Move with the wind of the Holy Spirit. We need to stop directing the wind and let the wind direct us. When we do this, and really yield to what he's doing, we will see what we are looking for.

God is looking for people who will let Jesus be the head, let the Holy Spirit move in the congregation, and let the Father's love pour out. We are the sheep, and he is the shepherd. We need to follow His voice. Follow the Shepherd.

Some people worry whether or not they are hearing His voice. They want to make sure that when they do feel something, that it really is Him. They spend so much time wavering and wondering that they miss out on the manifestations of His power, working in and through them.

If your spirit bears witness with His Spirit, then you need to trust that voice within your heart. You're not going to get out of line and cause distractions in the services, when God moves on you.

Listen, if it's the Holy Spirit, then it won't be a distraction.

But what if God wants to interrupt our patterns and way we "do church." I say, Lord distract us by the Holy Spirit! We need it! Get us out of our mind and into the Spirit. I love to be interrupted by the Holy Spirit. Don't you want to be interrupted by Him every day?

9

THE DARK HORSE MOVEMENT: 2020 AND BEYOND

I HAD A DREAM. I saw the Body of Christ split into three sections. I was speaking to all three by walking back and forth a great distance. I was telling them, "Whenever the message of the secret place is preached, I see the most miracles and healings."

As I was speaking, I fell into a trance, and the Lord took me into a vision. Now remember—this is still in the dream. I've never fallen into a trance in a dream before, so I knew I needed to really focus on what I saw.

I was shown a songbook, and on the cover was the year 1955. Then another songbook took its place, with the year 1959. And lastly, another songbook appeared, with the year 1965.

I came out of the trance, but I was still dreaming. I continued speaking to the church. I told them that before I gave the message on the secret place, we needed to wait for more people. They were flooding into the three sections, and I didn't want them to miss out on what God would say and do.

Sadly, quite a few became restless and tired of waiting, even though I encouraged them to stay. Some left.

Suddenly, people wanted to give offerings and help support what was happening. There was an opportunity for people to give—no offering message was needed, because the people were so happy to help in this move of God.

After that, just as I was about to begin the message, I woke up.

DECODING THIS DREAM

The three sections of the church represent three periods of time, or three waves of God—not past waves but present and future. The message of the secret place will be revived, and we will hear it being preached. Miracles and healings will follow. This is a decade of the heart being awakened to His great love.

The three years I saw are very key points. I had to do some research to figure out this riddle from God. He speaks in secret sometimes, because He wants us to figure it out. The Bible tells us:

"It's the glory of God to conceal a matter, but the glory of kings is to search out a matter" (Proverbs 25:2).

"The secret things belong to the LORD our God, but the things revealed belong to us and to our children forever, that we may do all the words of this law" (Deuteronomy 29:29 NKJV).

Let's look at these three years. The first was 1955. I discovered many things about the year 1955 that are significant because of the relationship to the other years I saw, 1959 and 1965. I knew that something revolutionary took place during these years. I thought about how I saw the years written on a songbook, so I researched the music of these years.

I found out that the genres of popular music changed drastically, beginning in 1955 with the rise of rock music. It remained the most popular genre until 1959, when soul music topped the charts. And soul music stayed the most popular music through 1965. God pointed to this music revolution from rock to soul, which had not been popular at all until the year 1959.

Why? What coincided in culture to cause such a drastic change in music popularity?

The Civil Rights Movement, from 1955-1965, was one of the key factors in the rise of soul music. It became the most popular genre of music in 1959.

A revolution started in 1955, when Rosa Parks rightfully refused to give up her seat on the bus in Montgomery, Alabama. Peaceful protests began and fueled the civil rights movement, which caused a needed cultural shift in the United States. A revolution was necessary, and it happened!

Along with this political awakening to truth, we see a direct effect on music. Soul music tops the charts during the Civil Rights Movement. Music helped fuel the passion, and the passion for civil rights fueled the music. This was a result of awakened hearts that were once asleep.

During the same time, God moved in tents across America! The Voice of Healing was at its peak during these years! Miracles swept America and the nations!

What is God saying?

There was a necessary awakening from 1955-1965, and we are at another necessary awakening now.

There will be three parts of this movement, as I saw three sections of people in the dream.

There will be an awakening of the heart as the Dark Horse Prophets come forth with miracles and healings, following their decrees to confirm the Word in the church, just as in the days of the voice of healing in the 50s and 60s. Their message will center on the intimacy found only at the cross of Jesus Christ. They will call people into the secret place of the Lord, where they will meet Him and be healed. As they minister, the Holy Spirit will move over the people and work wonders.

There will be an awakening in our justice system, and a civil rights movement for the unborn and children in slavery, just as we saw the civil rights movement for the injustice of racism. Corruption will be exposed, and truth shall be revealed. Justice is at hand.

There will be an awakening of the heart, as the Dark Horse Minstrels of music express in many genres a true heart for God. We will see hip-hop music continue to rise in popularity as a sign, just as soul music rose. It means a civil rights movement is at hand, and a miracle explosion in the church.

It will coincide with the pattern we saw from 1955-1965, which was a decade of awakening!

Once again, God is releasing an awakening to hearts and culture for this next decade. We will see the church, civil rights, and music shift with each other as a result of this new awakening. It is already happening. It has begun, and it will continue through 2030 and beyond.

We have seen a massive shift in the government of America. At the same time Trump became president, hip-hop music rose higher on the charts than ever before in history. It has now become the most popular genre of music in America.

Did you know that? Something is happening right before our eyes. God is using this genre, whether you like it or not, as a sign that the awakening is here, and God is establishing His government in every mountain of society. I believe we will see Christian hip-hop play a huge role and bring a massive harvest to Jesus.

I am convinced that this is what God is telling us through this dream and vision. I knew nothing about these years. I would not have dreamed this from my own imagination. This is why God uses riddles. So that we know for sure He has spoken. The Bible says, *"Surely the Lord GOD does nothing unless He reveals His secret counsel to His servants the prophets"* (Amos 3:7).

God always speaks of things to come before they happen. We must listen to His voice through His prophets.

"Believe in the LORD your God, and you shall be established; believe His prophets, and you shall prosper" (2 Chronicles 20:20, NKJV).

God continues to speak through the mouth of many prophets.

Do you hear His voice? Has God spoken of these things to you? Are you one of the dark horses? What has God called you to do for His Kingdom? Could you be one of the dark horse minstrels?

THE DARK HORSE MINSTRELS

The awakening of the dark horse minstrels is upon us now. A

minstrel is "a medieval singer or musician, especially one who sang or recited lyric or heroic poetry to a musical accompaniment for the nobility" (lexico.com). The Old French meaning is entertainer and servant.

I see God raising up His servants to perform for the King. They will not perform for the sake of being entertainers alone, but they will entertain the One True King, Jesus.

I had a dream in September, 2019. In that dream I saw Cindy Jacobs prophesy, "God is raising up His minstrels!" She spoke with authority, and the power of God rushed through me. They will rise from all over, known and unknown artists are being awakened.

Here's the word I released:

"God is raising up His minstrels! They will burn in the place of consuming fire, coming out of the cleft of the rock from the hidden places where they have met with God and have seen His glory. They will be fueled with resurrection power because of His great love, and they will go forth to reap a great harvest in the earth. God is raising up the minstrels to pour out true worship to their King, drawing many to encounter love itself, awakening a generation to the longing of God's heart. They will speak truth, out of a pure heart, and walk in righteousness.

Through their new song of the heart, many will see God. They will know the power of salvation, the truth of sonship, and the gift of righteousness. They will call forth repentance and weep before the people of God. They will be filled with awe and wonder. They will know the power of the Name of Jesus and His resurrection. They will see healings and miracles manifested as they worship.

They will draw attention only to the Son. They are the dark horses of God. And their sound will not be silenced."

They are coming. And they are here. They will have the sound of high praise in their mouths and most importantly in their hearts.

HIGH PRAISES

I saw the high praise sound coming forth in a greater way. This has begun. It began months after this next dream I want to share with you that God gave me.

This dream is about the high praises of God that will be released. This sound will come as the revelation that "Jesus is King" is released from the church. Only a few months after I prophesied this, Kanye West named his album "Jesus is King." I knew this confirmed that what I saw in this dream had indeed begun.

I had this dream on 12/12/2018. The date is very significant, because it is two twelves (twelve is apostolic and represents government).

I was worshiping at a meeting. I was standing with many believers up front, and there was a worship team playing slow music. It was a traditional service—it was the time of worship at the beginning. Everyone was standing up front.

But there was no wind on it, as we like to say sometimes. There was no power in it. Nothing moved me in its sound. It didn't lead me into the place in the Spirit that I wanted to go.

I want to go into the glory of God. I want to go into the realms of heaven. I want to get right into God's heart. I want to feel so close to him that it feels like he's pouring fire into my soul and spirit. I want to be so close to him that I feel intertwined like a woven blanket.

Do you know what I'm talking about? When you want to get to that intimate place but the worship music doesn't take you there? You may get frustrated, because the worship team is supposed to take you and usher you in. When they don't, then you've got to find a way to get there yourself.

In my dream, I could feel there was something more waiting for us. My spirit began to stir. I wanted to release praises to my God. I wanted to shout. I wanted to sing!

"THE UNDERGROUND SHEPHERD"

Just then, I noticed that Jerry Bryant stood directly in front of me. He's a pastor, known as the "Underground Shepherd," who shepherded the Father's blessing in Nashville after visiting Toronto in the 1990s. The outpouring of the Father's blessing had so much glory, miracles, and new sounds, especially the sound of high praise. I believe Jerry represents this: *the Father, a movement, a sound, a praise.*

Jerry was facing forward, toward the stage, and I was standing behind him. I reached my hands out to rest them on his shoulders (this is symbolic). I placed one hand on each shoulder. I seemed to be standing up higher somehow, as if I was on a stair step. Placing my hands on his shoulders seemed to release the sound I felt.

Just to note: Jerry has been a wonderful support and spiritual father to me and my husband, Munday Martin, over the years. I know that this dream is two-fold. Because of his support,

I will be able to release what is in my spirit. I will release a sound.

So my hands are resting on his shoulders. Scripture tells us "For unto us a Child is born, unto us a Son is given; and *the Government will be upon His shoulder. And His name will be called Wonderful, Counselor, Mighty God, Everlasting Father, Prince of Peace*" (Isaiah 9:6 NKJV). My hands were upon his shoulders, or the Government of Jesus. Because of this position, the foundation of Jesus Christ and His government, a new sound arose within me.

A NEW SONG

Immediately after placing my hands on his shoulders, a new song arose from my belly. I could feel it moving through me. Then out it came, louder than the sound in the room. Everyone could hear it:

"The Lord Most High! The Lord above the heavens! The Lord Most High! The Lord above the earth!"

I sang it over and over, full of high praise, joyful sounds and celebration. This revelation rose in my spirit:

"I know who my King is, I really know! He is above everything. I feel His majesty. I recognize His authority and power. I recognize His Government!"

I was singing from this place. The whole room listened.

Then, they caught it, like a wind. The worship team joined with me, as soon as they heard the words and the melody. They picked it right up, not missing a beat. The piano keys danced in delight. The sound became unified, and high praises rose to the King of kings.

The atmosphere in the place exploded. Everyone could feel it. It was as if we had to proclaim: "YOU ARE KING! YOU REIGN!"

It was electric. Freedom and dancing filled the room. Joy beamed on faces as we celebrated the good news that Jesus is King of all, He reigns supreme over the universe, and He has ultimate authority!

"Of the increase of His Government and peace there will be no end, upon the throne of David and over His Kingdom, to order it and establish it with judgment and justice from that time forward, even forever. The zeal of the Lord of hosts will perform this" (Isaiah 9:7 NKJV).

Did you hear that? The ZEAL of the Lord will perform this! Zeal for Him, passion for Him, true ecstatic praise for who He is! The zeal will produce His government on earth and in the heavens. We were getting it. *The Name of Jesus is truly above every other name.* Our troubles drifted away as we jumped and twirled, because the revelation of the King had come. It was the best party I've ever attended!

Then, because of tradition's strong hand, people began to go back to their seats. I mean, this is a meeting, right? We have stuff to do, and things to say. Our minds tell us that we must go on with the business at hand. It's time to do the next thing. I saw everyone leave the dance floor. The worship team went back into their traditional set.

I thought, "No! No! No! Please no!" and I began to rush to the microphone to say, "WAIT! Don't stop!"

My spirit was grieved. We had unified with the Father's heart in celebrating His Son. We were being adored by all of Heaven.

We were bringing so much joy to God; He loved it. It's all He really wants.

The dream ended with me pleading for the Body of Christ to stay —stay in the place of high praise.

"Stay there, and don't leave for anything! Not for tradition, not for your circumstances, and not because of what others are doing. Be the change. Be the breakthrough. Be the one who releases the high praises for Jesus!"

AWAKEN THE HEART OF HIGH PRAISE!

This year, I believe the Church will grab ahold of this. God is releasing the revelation of high praise. Those who hear His voice will know that He is saying this, and that He wants it more than anything.

God is going to release something in praise and worship that we've been missing, something we hunger for. We want freedom in the atmosphere of praise. We want to be taken up in a whirlwind. Something happens when true praise is released in a room, and we enter the glory of God.

Psalm 22:3 tells us that God inhabits the praises of His people. And 2 Corinthians 3:17 says, *"Now the Lord is the Spirit, and where the Spirit of the Lord is, there is liberty."*

We should feel so free when the Spirit of God is moving. I love to spin in the glory of God, and I want to be caught up in the clouds with Him. Don't you? Sometimes I literally feel as if I could float and dance upon the clouds with him. I felt that realm in the dream.

It's time to give Jesus the glory due to His name! It's time to enter into the revelation of the KING OF KINGS. He is here to establish His Kingdom on earth, through His people. This year is a time of activation. It's time to carry and release the new sound and authority of Jesus Christ to the world. The apostolic, governmental praise is here.

Jesus Christ is coming back! Let us proclaim: *"The King is coming...and His government will have no end!"*

God is speaking loud and clear. We will see three waves over this next decade, with the church bringing truth, the music bringing praise, and the government bringing justice. There will be an awakening of the heart with repentance, miracles, healings, and high praise in the church, an awakening of the heart expressed through song, and an awakening in our justice system.

We will look back after these next ten years and see a correlation of events that mirror the pattern of 1955, 1959, and 1965. Just as soul music rose quickly, and we saw the civil rights movement, so will the rise of hip-hop happening now coincide with a civil rights movement in the government. This will bring justice for all, including the unborn and children in slavery, all while a great outpouring of miracles and healings turns the church and world upside down for the glory of Jesus Christ. God has spoken and His Word never fails.

God is raising up His church, His minstrels, and His government. The Kingdom of heaven is at hand.

This is The Dark Horse Movement.

10

THE UNSTOPPABLE CALLING

I HAD an encounter with the Lord recently—He spoke to me about who I am. I felt the Holy Spirit speaking, his voice deep and strong in my spirit. He spoke clearly, and yet it is difficult to put into words what He said.

But I will try. And I pray the language of the Holy Spirit will speak to you. I pray that the river of His language will flow over you and into you, to communicate the same encouraging word of calling on your life that He gave to me.

GOD KNOWS WHO HE IS

Right now, he will come in and reveal to you his power, his authority, in a fresh way—He is the I AM. He spoke to Abraham in Genesis 17:1 and said, *"I am God Almighty."*

In Genesis 46:3 He said, *"I am God, the God of your father; do not be afraid to go down to Egypt, for I will make you a great nation there."*

He said to Joshua in Joshua 1:9, *"Have I not commanded you? Be strong and courageous! Do not tremble or be dismayed, for the LORD your God is with you wherever you go."*

And Jesus comforts us by saying in Matthew 28:20, *"I am with you always, even to the end of the age."*

God is always telling us that He is with us, always reminding us of who He is. He's always saying, "*I am* your God. *I am* your healer. *I am* your deliverer. *I am* your provider. *I am* your Savior. *I am* your Lord."

When God first came to Moses in Exodus 3:14, God said to Moses, *"I AM WHO I AM," and He said, "Thus you shall say to the sons of Israel, 'I AM has sent me to you.'"*

I love that the Lord referred to Himself as *I am*. Knowing the Lord's voice, and those two words, *I am*, I want this to speak to you. I want I AM to speak to you. I want you to hear His voice. Do not look at yourself, or what you have or what you can bring to the Lord. Instead, look at Him today and say, "God, you are! You are the I AM!"

In Genesis 15:1, God told Abraham, *"Do not fear, Abram, I am a shield to you; your reward shall be very great."*

He continues encouraging His children, Israel, all throughout their journey with Him. He says countless times, "*I am* your God." "*I am* the Lord your God who brought you out of Egypt." He reminds His people often of who He is and what He has done for them. In Genesis 31:13, He says, "*I am* the God of Bethel." Beth means house and el means God. He is the God of Bethel. The God of His own house. Throughout the Bible we notice God often precedes His directions with '*I am* the Lord," or "*I am* your God."

Before He speaks a word to his people He proclaims who He is.

JESUS KNOWS WHO HE IS

When Jesus Christ began his earthly ministry, He proclaimed who he was to people. Jesus boldly says that He is *I am.* In John 8:58, Jesus said, "Truly, truly, I say to you, before Abraham was born, *I am.*" In John 6:35, he says, "*I am* the bread of life." In John 10:11, he tells us, "*I am* the Good Shepherd." And, in John 8:12, he proclaims, "*I am* the Light of the world."

He doesn't stop there! In John 14:6, Jesus says, *"I am the way, and the truth, and the life."* In John 15:5 he declares, *"I am the vine, you are the branches."* And in John 11:25, he says, *"I am the resurrection and the life."*

In Luke 4:18 (NKJV), He stood up in the midst of a crowd and proclaimed who he is. Even in the midst of those who would not receive Him. They did not accept what He had to say, nor who He was, yet He stood strong before their faces without wavering. Jesus stood up in the synagogue for the reading of the day, and He read, *"The Spirit of the LORD is upon Me, Because He has anointed Me To preach the gospel to the poor; He has sent Me to heal the brokenhearted, To proclaim liberty to the captives And recovery of sight to the blind, To set at liberty those who are oppressed"*

He knows who He is and what He was born to do.

Jesus, in all of his humility, gentleness and meekness, rode on the donkey into Jerusalem, as the King of kings and Lord of lords. He was born in a manger, the most humble of beginnings, in a barn with animals. It smelled. It was cold and uncomfortable. The lowest and poorest of places, and yet here is Jesus, the King of all.

Jesus knows who He is.

THE APOSTLE PAUL KNEW WHO HE WAS
...DO YOU KNOW WHO YOU ARE?

Let's look at the Apostle Paul for a bit. Paul seemed to know who he was. He said in Galatians 2:20 (KJV), "*I am* crucified with Christ. Nevertheless, I live; yet not I, but Christ liveth in me."

Paul knew who he was and who he used to be. Then, he died to it. He crucified it with Christ. You also must come to that place of identifying with Christ in the crucifixion. Like Paul, only then can we know who we really are and what we are called to do.

First, identify what you are dead to, and what you are *not* called to anymore. Understand what you used to be, and what you are no longer. Identify with the cross—you are dead to sin, cleansed by the blood, forgiven and set free from your old nature.

> "*Therefore, if anyone is in Christ, he is a new creation; old things have passed away; behold, all things have become new*" (2 Corinthians 5:17 NKJV).

Who are you? You are dead to sin. Do you know who you are? Do you know that you're forgiven, cleansed by the blood, and dead to your old nature, if you have truly repented? You're dead to the old ways and dead to the power of that flesh. *That is who you are.*

First, I am crucified with Christ. Just as the Father

proclaimed, "I am the Lord God Almighty," And Jesus said, "I am the Anointed One," we need to stand in the presence of the Lord and say, "I am crucified with Christ, old things are passed away, all things are new in me."

Who am I? "I am dead to sin."

Paul knew this, and he knew the one that he had been born into—Christ alone. He knew the one who had suffered. He knew the fellowship of those sufferings. Do you know the fellowship of his sufferings? Have you come to know Christ through the things you have suffered in your life? Do you know him and the power of his resurrection?

What comes after the suffering? What comes after the death? What comes after the crucifixion of the works of the flesh, which have manifested in your life until that day that you became crucified with Christ? What comes after is the power of the Spirit of Resurrection through the Holy Spirit working in you, raising you up, and making you alive in him.

In Philippians 3:10, Paul says *"that I may know Him and the power of His resurrection and the fellowship of His sufferings, being conformed to His death."* We will only know Christ, and know who we truly are, when we no longer live for ourselves. We must die to self, the old self crucified on the cross with Jesus, and become the last not the first.

God knows who He is. God doesn't have a problem knowing who He is, and He's not prideful about it. He is full of grace and humility. It's not prideful for you to know who you are. You have been made in His image, and you are like Him. Some might say that it's prideful to say "I am this" or "I am that."

The Bible does say, *"Let another praise you, and not your own mouth"* (Proverbs 27:2). While that is true, we are not praising ourselves when we proclaim who we are in Christ. Knowing who I am is very different from praising myself.

The Father knows who he is. Jesus knows who he is. And Jesus, by the Holy Spirit coming and baptizing us, making us a new creation, is now on a mission to cause us to know who we are in him. Just as he appeared to Paul (then living as the old man, Saul) on the road to Damascus to let him know who he was, he does the same for us. He's conforming us unto his death. He wants us to understand that we must become dead to the power of that flesh nature, dead to the power of sin. We must completely become crucified to it through the power of the Holy Spirit.

Paul writes in Romans 8:13, *"For if you are living according to the flesh, you must die; but if by the Spirit you are putting to death the deeds of the body, you will live."*

Focus on those words, *by the Spirit.* Jesus always reminds us that apart from Him we can do nothing, so, deny yourself, pick up your cross, and follow Him.

When you realize that you are dead to sin and alive in Christ, the power of the enemy has no hold over you, just like it has no hold over Jesus. Jesus is alive! Now you are alive, in Christ! You are completely risen in Christ, with the power of the Resurrection working in you. Paul knew this. Paul knew Christ. He knew suffering. He knew resurrection. And he knew what death was. He knew what true death was.

Pray this right now:

Father, help me know what true death is—death to myself, death to the power of sin, death to allowing the illusions of the enemy to parade around in my mind anymore. Help me know that I am dead to all that, and it has no power over my life. May I become dead to this world, dead to everything that has no truth in it. No life in it. No light in it. May I become dead to it right now. Lord, crucify me, crucify those things, with you. I thank you that it has already been done, and I ask for the Spirit of Revelation. In Jesus' name. Amen.

In Romans 6:11, Paul comes to a place where he says, *"I reckon myself to be dead to sin but alive unto God through Jesus Christ our Lord."*

I want to ask you this right now. Have you come to this place of reckoning? Within yourself, can you say that you are dead to your old nature? Dead to the things you used to identify with, that labeled you in your mind and your thoughts and your emotions? Dead to who you were, who the world fashioned you to be, who life told you to be? Have you reckoned that all of that is now dead? If you are dead to all of that, then it no longer has power over you!

You must believe and reckon within yourself that you are dead to that, and you are alive unto God through Jesus Christ our Lord. Hallelujah!

We've died to everything else, just like Paul. And what comes after death in Christ? Resurrection! When you've died to something in Christ, right on the other side of that death is resurrection power! The power of the Resurrection in Christ comes upon Paul, and he receives the understanding that he was made alive to God. He knew who he was. He knew it to the point that he began to proclaim it.

This is what the power of the resurrection does in you. When you've died and become crucified with Christ, and you let that resurrection power, the voice of the Holy Spirit, work in you, the voice of living water will make you new every day. There are new mercies every day, reminding you that all the old things have passed away. All the old flesh is dead. You wake up with new mercies. You wake up in resurrection power every day, and miracles are waiting for you.

"All things are possible with God" is waiting for us every single morning that we get up. You must know that you can be in this place. Say it now—"*I am* walking in the resurrected power of Jesus!" Say it every morning when you wake up.

You are going to rise up every day free from all the patterns of the old nature that tormented you. Free from insecurity. Free from fear. Free from failure. Free from anger and offense. Free from unforgiveness. You are going to crucify them daily on the cross.

Don't allow old emotional patterns, because of circumstances or how you've been raised, to remain alive. We tend to make these excuses. "Well, I'm just this way because my parents were this way," or, "Well, I'm just this way because I went through this trauma." While this is completely understandable, and might be true, I have Good News for you. Jesus surpasses all of that! His is the name above every name. If you will give it to Him, He will make you triumph over those things. He bore them on the cross for you! And that is where they died.

When we come into Christ, we become crucified with him, and we become free from those things. They are dead to us. If we recognize that they are dead, they cannot manifest fruit in us anymore. We have to *know* that we *know* that we *know this*.

The Father knows who He is.

Jesus knows who He is.

And you are alive in Christ.

When you rise up in the morning, identify with the resurrected Christ, and don't identify with the crucified works of the flesh.

Paul knew this. Filled with the Spirit of Truth, he prophesied in 1st Timothy 2:7, *"For this I was appointed a preacher and an apostle (I am telling the truth, I am not lying) as a teacher of the Gentiles, in faith and truth."* He declares his true identity, just like the Father and Jesus declare, "I am! I am the Almighty God. I am the God of Abraham, Isaac, and Jacob. I am the Lord Almighty. I am that I am."

Paul confirmed himself as three different offices; a preacher, an apostle, and a teacher. He was confident in what God called him to do, and he said it. He spoke it and proclaimed it, because he was in agreement with the Holy Spirit.

Begin to proclaim, "I am in Christ! The Anointed One is in me! The *I am* is in me, and because of that, I can proclaim by the voice of the Holy Spirit, who has anointed me—I am called to be a prophet, I am called to teach, I am called to pray for the sick, I am called to prophesy in the church. I am called to prophesy in the streets. I am called to evangelize the nations. I am called to speak at churches. I am called to teach in schools. I am called!

Can you say that today? Don't allow false humility to rob you of your calling, a false humility that ignores who you are in the power of Jesus Christ.

Remain humble in your heart before the Lord, knowing it is He who has empowered you with these gifts and callings. But at the same time, be assured of who you are. The Lord knows your heart. If somebody hears you say, "I'm a prophet, I'm a teacher," or "I have a pastoral anointing," and people think that you're saying it in pride, then here's what you say—"God knows my heart, and I'm speaking truth."

Paul said, "I'm speaking the truth and I'm not lying." Let them know what you're called and anointed to do—not with a spirit of pride, but in godly humility. True humility acknowledges the truth and proclaims it. It's time to stop wavering on that boat, tossing to and fro, wondering whether or not you're called and anointed. I hear the Lord saying, "Stop it today, and start proclaiming who you are."

Are you ready to accept once and for all who you are in Christ?

11

THE RELEASE OF THE DARK HORSES

THE SCRIPTURE SAYS in Philippians 1:6, *"For I am confident of this very thing, that He who began a good work in you will perfect it until the day of Christ Jesus."*

Do you hear that? He who has started the work within you, what He has put inside of you, what He created you to be before even the world was formed, will be perfected. He knew you, and He knew His plans for you before you were put into your mother's womb. You were in His mind before the world was even created, because He is not bound by time. He said He knew you before He formed you. Think about that. Before He created your spirit He knew everything about you. Before He put you in your mother's womb, He anointed you and called you.

Jeremiah 1:5 says, *"Before I formed you in the womb I knew you. And before you were born I consecrated you; I have appointed you a prophet to the nations."* That is God speaking to Jeremiah. But God is no respecter of persons. He has done the same for you.

Before you were born, God put your calling within you, in

your spirit, before you became a person living on earth. Before you ever identified with what your life and your circumstances told you about yourself, God said something different. Don't accept that old false identity. It is not what you were created to do—it was not your calling from the beginning.

The enemy and the flesh will try to manipulate and confuse you, creating false images of fear, unbelief, anxiety, stress, anger, depression, or hopelessness. Those are false images, and they are not true. They may be part of your current story, but God gave you a different story long before. Believe God's story. The others are lies. We must chop those lies off right now.

You were created in the image of Christ. Before you ever became flesh and blood—that is the real and eternal you. That's who you are, that's what you identify with, and that's why it becomes so alive in you when Jesus speaks to you. When the Spirit of Truth comes and speaks to you, and talks to you about your calling, it becomes alive in you.

Your baby starts bouncing. Your spirit starts bouncing, because you know who you are, and you recognize it in His Presence. You're reminded when the anointing comes upon you, and you remember who you are.

The Lord will come to us over and over. He will prophesy the truth to us until we believe the truth about ourselves. God has spoken to us and He is never going to stop. He never gives up.

He is asking you today:

Are you ready to start proclaiming who I created you to be, before you were ever born on this earth? Are you ready to be confident in this very thing?

FOUND IN CHRIST

You are found in Christ. You were called to be within Christ before the foundations of the world. When you are born again and receive Jesus as Lord and Savior, you become a new creation, joined into Christ, restored back to him as the purified spirit you were created to be. He forgives you, because you have believed in Him and received what He has done for you. Everything's removed, old things have passed away and you are purified through the Holy Spirit, who conforms you into the image of Christ.

You are literally joined with His Spirit, so you are inside Christ Himself. He existed before the foundations of the world. When we come into Christ, we are outside of time, beyond the barriers of the identity bound by our earthly existence. We are not defined by our experiences here, when we've been born into a new and living way, found in the dimensions of Christ.

This life is but a moment that exists in the eternity of who you are in Christ. The moments that hurt you and brought great trauma, causing you to walk in anger, fear, depression, and pain, formed you into a false image, different from who the Spirit of Truth says you are. It pulled you outside of the light and pushed you into darkness. But you are still that image of God on the inside of your heart, deep down. You are His, and your heart knows that and longs to return to His heart, the place where you were made.

These moments of separation are but a vapor of time, and you don't have to stay there trapped inside that darkness. It has no power over the truth in you, which is eternal. Let Jesus have those moments. He will heal you and remind you who you truly are.

His anointing is beyond time. It breaks every yoke of bondage to set you free. Give in to Jesus. He is the Anointed One. The great I am. He is saying to you, right now, "I am healer. I am provider. I AM in you! The one who was, and is, and is to come, in you!"

There is an eternal realm that exists within you. This means that you can operate outside the limitations of this flesh realm, if you believe in Him. You are a spirit being. You call those things that are not as though they were. You cause manifestations in the creation of things that are supposed to be, because you identify with the Spirit of Truth within you. You start calling forth those things to manifest in the earth.

The Lord is opening your eyes, helping you to see beyond what you've experienced in your life. He wants you to see beyond all memories. You're so much bigger, so much greater, so much more beautiful, than how the pain shaped you. You're more precious, and so much more amazing.

Your spirit is strong in God, but the flesh is weak. That's why we can say, "In my weakness, I'm strong. When I am weak, I am strong. The flesh is weak, but in your spirit you are strong.

I had a dream recently. I saw miracles in a hospital, and people were excited about how much power and faith they felt to pray for others. Even though I felt weak, I saw miracles when I prayed for the sick. The group that was with me, were also seeing miracles as they prayed, and were smiling and full of faith. I said, "Don't you understand? It's in our weakness that He is made strong!" I wept as this revelation of His mercy that moves through our weakness overtook me. The power of God is found in our weakness. I knew our weakness is the greatest way for Him to reveal his glory and mercy. It's the place we recognize we have total dependence on him and not ourselves. It was a beautiful moment. I was overwhelmed with his presence.

You are strong because you are in Christ. It's time to start saying, "I am in Christ." What does that look like? What does it mean to be in Christ?

I'll tell you what it doesn't look like. It doesn't look like depression. It doesn't look like fear. It doesn't look like insecurity.

These are some of the things that try to stop you from stepping out into what God has shown you to do. Nothing can stop the calling of God on your life. Not one thing, and not one person, can stop the calling of God on your life.

Except you. You are the only one who can stop it, and that's if you choose not to go after it.

Isaiah 43:10-13 (NKJV): "You are My witnesses," says the
Lord, "And My servant whom I have chosen,
That you may know and believe Me,
And understand that I am He.
Before Me there was no God formed,
Nor shall there be after Me.
I, even I, am the Lord,
And besides Me there is no savior.
I have declared and saved,
I have proclaimed,
And there was no foreign god among you;
Therefore, you are My witnesses,"
Says the Lord, "that I am God.

Indeed, before the day was, I am He;
And there is no one who can deliver out of My hand;
I work, and who will reverse it?"

Did you hear that? This is the Lord speaking through his prophet Isaiah, and He says that before anything ever existed, before the day was even created, He said, "I am."

We're talking about a powerful God. This is what I want you to grab right now. The magnificent God who is *I am*. He is your God and your Father, and you are His child. You are a child of God. I want you to get this. You are a child of this Eternal Being who exists outside of all creation. "Before the day was, I am He."

There is none that can deliver out of his hand. When He has grabbed you, and you are in His hand, there is nothing that can take you out of it. He said, *"Be strong and courageous, do not be afraid or tremble at them, for the LORD your God is the one who goes with you. He will not fail you or forsake you" (Deuteronomy 31:6).*

With his own right hand He brought salvation. The power of his right hand, who is Jesus Christ, at the right hand of the Father, the Savior of all, the Lord of lords, the Kings of kings, the one whom you believe, the one who has saved you, who makes intercession for you, is in you.

And you are in Christ. You are held by the right arm of God. You are in his hands, and because you're in His hand, He says there is none that can deliver out of His hand. None! Nobody! Not one thing can stop the anointing and calling on your life, because in the next part of that Scripture, Isaiah 43:13 (NKJV), He says, *"I work, and who can reverse it?"*

When you are in the hand of God, God closes you within that hand, and He uses His hands to create. He said, "I will work." Oftentimes He makes something to move and shake you. It may feel like you are breaking.

We may say, "God is breaking me." Especially when we go through really tough times. And I get it, because I've been there, and sometimes it felt like I lived there. It felt like I was breaking, being crushed, suffocating.

But I was shown what is actually happening to us in these times. Our God is the great potter, and we are the clay on the potter's wheel. While a potter is shaping and forming his creation, at what point does He break it? Why would someone, who is putting all their heart into this clay, actually get fed up, take it off the wheel, and break it? I can't imagine anyone would, and neither does our God.

What feels like breaking is the making! You think you're being crushed, but you're actually being formed and molded. You think you're being suffocated, but you're being held by the potter's hands. You are exactly where you're supposed to be.

Don't jump off the wheel! Yield to His hands. Trust Him. And the entire time His eye is on you. Make sure you are patient and allow him to form you into the work He's imagined in His heart.

This process is precious to Him.

God is asking us to stop saying that we are broken. We are never broken, but in the process of *becoming*. We are being conformed into the image of his Son.

That's not breaking, it's making!

I could feel the deep sincerity of our Father as He shared His heart with me about this. He never does destructive acts to you, or to any of His children. It grieves Him when we use this term "breaking."

He is always at the potter's wheel, working on you, and when you're ready, He puts you in the fire. Not to burn you, but to complete you. And nothing can ever break you again, because He finished the work. It is done! And He has placed you into the fire of His Holy Spirit, who seals you forever. And you come out shining!

He is forming you, He is working. Who can reverse it? When He breathed you into being, like He did Adam, He created your spirit, along with everything you were called and anointed to do. You came, filled with all the promises of God within you, ready to manifest and be created.

When the Lord spoke the universe into existence, the universe began to expand. Did you know—to this day the universe is still expanding, because of the creative power of God?

This gives us a picture for our own life. When God speaks something into existence it always increases—it's not a limited space. There are no boundaries. You are meant to multiply and increase. You might think you are at the end of your journey, and this is as far as it's going to go.

"Is this the extent of what I'm going to see God do in my life?"

But that would be against the very nature of the Lord. When He speaks something forth, like when He told Adam and Eve go and multiply and replenish the earth, He said, "Multiply." That word is still alive today. Have you noticed—the world population only increases? It's the principle of multiplication that God released in the Spirit. It's going to multiply and multiply and multiply. There's no end to the multiplication. There's no decrease to the multiplication. There's no stopping the multiplication.

Isaiah 55:11 says, *"So will My word be which goes forth from My mouth; it will not return to Me empty, without accomplishing what I desire, and without succeeding in the matter for which I sent it."*

His word cannot fail. Therefore, you cannot fail. You are in that Word that He sent into the earth. You have gone forth from His mouth and you will not return empty, void, or fruitless, without accomplishing the purpose that God created you for. Have faith in God. Have faith in His Word. You will not fail.

The Bible says, *"Now He who supplies seed to the sower and bread for food will supply and multiply your seed for sowing and increase the harvest of your righteousness"* (2 Corinthians 9:10).

Whatever seed is sown is the crop that multiplies. If we sow apple seeds, we see apples multiplied. God increases the fruit that I produce in my life. What is that fruit? Galatians 5:22, 23, "The fruit of the Spirit is love, joy, peace, patience, kindness, goodness, faithfulness, gentleness, self-control; against such things there is no law."

We sow this fruit when we minister to others. God is faithful to increase it as we go. Start with a small mustard seed if you have to. Use that little act of love and kindness, and give it away to someone who needs it. Then watch God multiply that seed. He will bring you more people who are in need, and He will meet the needs you have. Take care of His business, and He will take care of yours.

There is no limitation. There is no box. There is an ever-increasing multiplication of fruit in your life, because that is how the spirit realm works. You will not go backwards. You are forever moving forward. Romans 11:29 says, *"For the gifts and the calling of God are irrevocable."* They are without repentance, which means turning away from. You cannot turn from them and go the other direction. You can't reverse it. Your enemies can't reverse it. No one can reverse it. The devil can't reverse it. It's not going to be stopped, because of the creative power of God's voice. You are forever going to increase, even into eternity. For all time there's going to be an increase of fruit from you, which will bring glory to Jesus Christ.

In Revelation 22:13, Jesus says, *"I am the Alpha and Omega, the first and the last, the beginning and the ending."* And in Revelation 1:8 He says, *"...which is and which was and which is to come."*

The Almighty One wants you to know, because you are in Him, there is much to come in your life. Jesus started the work, and He's finishing the work. He says, "Do not be afraid, for I am with you, wherever you go now."

With that in mind, I want to challenge you today:

1. Know who He is, know who you are, and know you are dead to sin. Identify with that nature—you're dead to all that stuff that the world has tried to put on you, or that life has tried to put on you. It cannot influence your future. You are dead to those things. They have no power over you, and they will not manifest fruit.

2. Identify with the power of resurrection of Jesus Christ in you that is increasing the fruit of your calling and your anointing to the world.

3. Choose to move forward and obey what God has spoken to you.

All the things that you set on the shelf, the things that you feared beginning, let all the excuses go and be confident today in what you've been called to do. Out of respect for the Holy Spirit, and in obedience to God, choose once and for all to say "yes" to your calling.

He wants to see you fulfill everything He has prophesied into your life. He wants to see it, and if you know that all of heaven is backing you, would you step out of the boat today and onto the water? Go to Jesus. He will always provide for you. He will hold you up. He will make the way straight every time. He will come and work alongside you. He will always be with you wherever you go.

Will you make the decision right now? Let the fear of God, a reverential awe of His mighty power and unending love, come on you, out of respect for His great authority, respect for who He is, the Creator of the universe, the Lord of lords and King of kings.

Let us say together, "I will Lord! Whatever you say, I will do it!"

The fear of the Lord is the beginning of wisdom. Let that propel you into your calling. If we don't answer, if we don't choose to step out of the boat and go after everything God has put within us, if we keep holding back, letting the cloak of the flesh dictate our actions because of the fear of men's faces or fear of failure, then we will miss out on His beautiful rewards in our lives.

The Lord doesn't want that. But we can miss out on the blessings He has for us, if we choose not to allow Him to work through us. The good news is, as long as we come into agreement with His anointing, with who we are in Christ Jesus, we will receive every blessing He wants to shower on us. Step out of the boat. Come into agreement with His calling. Start stepping out and doing what He's told you to do.

When you do that, you're going to see so much blessing poured over your life. Everything that He wants to multiply and increase to you, He's going to start giving that to you. You're going to see multiplication happen every step you take.

Acknowledge who you are. Be confident in what He has told you and do it!

Let's pray.

Father I thank you for who you are, and I thank you for who I am in Christ Jesus. I feel the encouragement of your voice. I pray for the Spirit of Truth right now to quicken me, to lead me, to guide me into the purpose and calling you have planned for me. I thank you that I hear and know your voice, and I follow you. Lord, break every lie and every attempt of the enemy that tries to stop me from moving forward. Let the fire of your Holy Spirit come upon me. Help me to know your voice and your deep love for me.

You are for me and not against me. I know that nothing can stop me when you are on my side. No one can take me out of your hand or reverse the work that you have begun. I will not wear another identity—only the one you have given me. I step out of the old nature and into the new identity in Christ. Let the fear of the Lord come upon me as I humble myself to you. I thank you for giving me faith by the Holy Spirit, for giving me a spirit of boldness to proclaim the gospel of Jesus Christ to every living creature. In Jesus' name. Amen.

Declare this today!

I am called.

I am anointed.

I am chosen by God

I am called to preach.

I am called to teach.

I am called to start a business.

I am called to be an artist.

I am called to write books.

I am called to start a business and run companies.

I am anointed to do whatever I'm called to do.

I am called to speak.

I am called to sing.

I am called to pray.

I am called to come into agreement with the Lord God and the Holy Spirit.

I am called to shift situations in the Spirit.

I am called to the prayer closet.

I am called to the secret place.

I am called to the streets.

I am called to evangelism.

I am called to the nations.

I am called to prophesy to the lost and see them come home.

I am called to the prodigal.

I am called to the sheep.

I am called to sons and daughters.

I am called to children.

I am called to the elders of the church to encourage them.

I am called as a father to the church.

I am called as a mother to the church.

I am called to my family.

I am called as a pillar of faith.

I am called to pray and cover my family in the Blood of Jesus Christ.

I am called to rescue children.

I am called to lay down my life for Jesus.

Come on! What are you called to? Speak it out right now.

Whatever it is that you're called to, do it. Agree with it and proclaim it.

It may be many of these things, or something unique that I did not mention. There are endless possibilities, because God is creative, omnipotent, and limitless. Nothing is impossible with God!

Because He wants to fill all things with his glory, the church should be spread out in the marketplace, in the streets, and in all the venues of business and every cultural activity in the earth. The church is to be woven into all of it, to bring light in the darkness.

Remind yourself who you are consistently. Rise up and declare today,

I am called. I am anointed. I am a dark horse.

Be on the lookout for the next installment of *The Awaken Collection* by Jennifer Martin—written to take you on a continued journey unto an awakened heart.

MEET THE AUTHOR

Jennifer Martin and her husband, Munday, are the founders of Contagious Love International. They are prophetic healing evangelists based in the Nashville, TN area, where they are raising their two children.

Jennifer and Munday are committed to preaching the gospel of Jesus Christ to America and the nations, equipping a supernatural Jesus generation who will manifest miraculous lives to impact communities and culture. They both minister and preach in the Glory, blazing a trail of reformation, miracles, healings, signs and wonders, and intense outbreaks of the glory of God in churches, conferences, crusades, and the streets in the US and the nations, leading many into the fullness of God.

They emphasize on loving the lost in the nations and inspiring others to do so through acts of compassionate love. They started their ministry living in Israel for nearly a year in a total of 20 trips to the Holy Land serving the people of Israel and working with and encouraging the body of Christ in Israel while ministering to the lost on the streets. They are hoping to pioneer a grassroots movement in the church marked by believers living a life in the fullness of God by knowing their seat of authority in

Christ, who they are in the word of God, and one basked in the wonder and amazement of loving God and society around them. They are teaching a generation to believe for the impossible by fully embracing the gospel of Jesus Christ, and rising in their God given authority in his word to disciple nations as sons and daughters of the King.

Munday and Jennifer's belief is simple- God's grace and love is for all mankind through His Son Jesus! The go of the gospel means go! They hope to ignite and inspire the church's need to arise into a lifestyle of evangelism for harvesting nations. Not only do they preach it, but they model it in their everyday lives.

Munday and Jennifer have traveled the globe extensively in 28 nations seeing literally thousands come to Christ through international crusade work, missions, creative & power street evangelism, and churches since 1999. They have a passion to make disciples, a desire to see a supernatural Jesus generation rise up who will promote transformation & counter cultural reformation through intimacy with the Holy Spirit. Most importantly, they long to make Christ relevant to this post modern society. Jennifer and Munday have been commissioned by Prophet James Goll of Encounters Network, author of countless books including "The Seer, The Discerner, and The Prophet." Jennifer and Munday were both ordained in 2009 by Jeff Jansen of Global Fire Ministries, author of "Glory Rising." Munday and Jennifer also are now active members of Jeff Jansen's Global Connect under the leadership of Jeff Jansen and Chuck Pierce, and Munday and Jennifer are also members of Che Ahn's apostolic network called H.I.M., a coalition of church leaders and ministries around the world.

Contagious Love International's Board of Apostolic Advisors

- James Goll of *Encounters Network*
- Mickey Robinson of *Prophetic Destiny International*
- Pastor Jerry Bryant Nashville Tennessee

For more information visit:
www.contagiousloveintl.com